The Freedom of

Forgiveness

John Arcovio

Cover art work by John Arcovio.

All scripture quotations are from the King James Version of the Holy Bible unless noted.

The Freedom of Forgiveness by John S. Arcovio
Published by Spirit Led Ministries Publishing
©2008

Printed in the United States of America.
First printing July, 2008

ISBN 978-0-9647343-5-7

For more information on other materials by John Arcovio, or to reorder materials, please contact:

Spirit Led Ministries, Inc.
slmpub@aol.com
www.spiritled.org

Acknowledgments
Scripture Text

Scripture Text

Mark 11:25

25 And when ye stand praying, forgive, if ye have ought against any: that your Father also which is in heaven may forgive you your trespasses.

1
The Freedom of Forgiveness

I firmly believe that we are in a Solomon type of revival, a revival of repentance, intimacy and restoration of the Glory of God. II Chronicles 7 :11 records, "If my people, which are called by my name," (we have been called by His mighty name.) – "shall humble themselves," that's repentance – "and pray," (that's relationship with God) – "and seek my face," (that's the second mile of intercession, going beyond interceding and going on into intercession) – "and turn from their wicked ways;" (the final act of true, heart rending, changing repentance) – "then will I hear from heaven," (that's the beginning of the outpouring) – "and will forgive their sin and heal their land."

The phrase "heal their land," I believe, is where we're at right now, the resident anointing that results from inner healing and restoration of the Glory of God.

There are things you can step into in the Holy Ghost now and then. There are things you can touch in the Holy Ghost now and then. But what we're seeking for is that *resident* anointing. This is an anointing that is with us from day to day, not just a flash in the pan on Sunday night or Wednesday night and back into trouble, discouragement, and bondage the next day, but *resident* anointing! This is a daily walking and *living* in the Spirit. This is the dimension of the revelation of the Glory of God in the lives of those who reverence and fear the Lord. This was the shadow, (which I believe was a manifestation of the Glory of God), that was recorded in Acts 5:15, "Insomuch that they brought forth the sick into the streets, and laid them on beds and couches, that at the least the shadow of Peter passing by might overshadow some of them." Peter walked in the daily *resident anointing*. This is why the Glory of God was so strong and evident in the lives of the first church.

For the church in this hour to be able to step into that resident anointing there has to be a healing. God said, "I will *heal* their land." The decision to forgive facilitates this healing.

When this principle was first shown to me, I had to go through it several times in order to grasp an understanding of it. As with most revelations, I could repeat them from my mind as facts, and even preach them, but until I received them engrafted into my spirit, then the true power of the revelation did not work in my life. The power of the revelation of the freedom of forgiveness it is unprecedented. I pray that we'll be able to grasp what God desires to do in our lives. This can only be facilitated from the freedom of forgiveness.

Forgiveness will allow you to conquer, overcome and destroy the yoke of shame. Shame is probably one of the biggest hindrances in a child of God's walk. Why? Shame will keep you from doing what you should more than anything else. Shame can be defined as- *the feeling of loss of respect from someone of significance or by yourself over a mistake or seeming failure committed.* Shame will tell you somehow you are defective; you will never get to where the Spirit wants you because of a poor choice made in life. Jesus shed His blood on Calvary so we might be free from the chains of shame and lay claim to the promise of the prophet Joel recorded in Joel 2:26-27, "And you shall eat in plenty and be satisfied and praise the name of the Lord, your God, Who has dealt wondrously with you. And *My people shall never be put to shame.* 27 And you shall know, understand, and realize that I am in the midst of Israel and that I the Lord am your God and there is none else. *My people shall never be put to shame.*"[i] (EMPHASIS MINE)

In the freedom of forgiveness, chains of shame can be unlocked. When you step out and try to be used of God, sometimes the enemy comes to try and remind you of your past failures to keep you from your future and full potential. In the freedom of forgiveness, there are no "skeletons" in your closet of life, only trophies of His grace!

I believe we've reached a point in God, in this move of God, in this time of the Holy Ghost, that God wants to begin to move in *resident* anointing. I'm not talking about the devil fighting us, because the devil's power is limited. He was defeated at Calvary. Jesus spoke of this stripping of the enemies armor(power) in Luke 11:20-22, "But if I with the finger of God cast out devils, no doubt the kingdom of God is come upon you. 21 When a strong man armed keepeth his palace, his goods are in peace: 22 But when a stronger than he shall come upon him, and overcome him, he taketh from him all his armour wherein he trusted, and divideth his spoils." The armor was power Satan held over the people of God.

When we choose to hold grudges and harbor bitterness, we give the power Jesus stripped from the enemy back to him. This principle is seen recorded in

2 Corinthians 2:10-11, "To whom ye forgive any thing, I forgive also: for if I forgave any thing, to whom I forgave it, for your sakes forgave I it in the person of Christ;11 Lest *Satan should get an advantage of us*: for we are not ignorant of his devices." (EMPHASIS MINE)

I'm talking about being empowered to accomplish what God has called and anointed us to do.

Unforgiveness is probably one of the most powerful tools that the devil uses. Paul said, "Be not ignorant of the devil's devices." Sometimes some people are vastly ignorant of the devil's devices. We don't want to be ignorant, but we want to become equipped. We don't want to give the enemy advantage in spiritual warfare; we want to take the advantage! At times you absolutely feel like you cannot forgive a situation, a person and the truth is, within our human ability, this is impossible. However, God can empower us to forgive and love people we never thought we could thru His *agape love*.

I remember a time when I was about nineteen years old. I had given myself back over to God completely in desperate seeking to draw near to Him, and I was fasting and praying to know Him in a deeper, more intimate manner. I mean, I was fasting days, even weeks and praying hours after hours seeking

God's face. There seemed to be a barrier, a block. I lived under condemnation and guilt. I lived under bondage. I couldn't feel liberty. I would get victory in a service, but then it would vanish the next morning.

Then one night my pastor preached a very simple message on the root of bitterness, and the Holy Ghost began to speak to me about forgiveness. It seemed as if God pushed His big fingers on the area of my heart I had not submitted to him. It became very apparent to me through revelation of the Spirit that I could never truly come to a deeper, more intimate walk with the Lord unless I chose to forgive and release the things I was holding onto. I was waiting for someone to apologize or attempt to make the things that had gone terribly wrong, right but the Spirit was urging me to forgive regardless if these things ever came to pass.

My brother, sister and I were raised by a very wounding step-father. I won't go into the whole horrific story now, but he was an ordained minister who abused us children physically. Because these horrific abuses occurred in a spirit filled pastor's home, my heart filled with bitterness and hatred against the ministry.

God spoke to me and said, "This is as far as you're going to go, John Arcovio." You can fast until your belly button falls off, but it won't help. Pray all night if you want to, but it won't get you anywhere! Memorize every Scripture in the Bible, if you please! "You won't go any higher than this until you release that bitterness and forgive!"

You can try to get around it; you can try, but you can't. Your freedom in Christ is tied to the freedom of forgiveness. I remember the day when the Spirit prompted me to call my step father and forgive him. I picked up the phone and called. When he answered I said, "Ray? I forgive you for everything . . . everything." What did "everything" mean? Ten years of insult and inhumane treatment. Ten years of physical beatings. Ten years of mental abuse. – just on and on and on. I have vowed to myself I would never forgive my step father, but, on that day under the leading and empowerment of the Spirit, I completely forgave him. The moment I said that to him, the Holy Ghost whispered to me, "The sky's the limit now! Nothing's going to stop you!" I challenge you to choose today to forgive and forget. The person who wounded you may even be dead and gone but if you will sit down and write them a letter, listing exactly what they did against you and then pray, "Father, today I choose to forgive _____ and completely release them from the harm they caused me." Now close your letter telling this person you have completely forgiven and released them.

Forgive! *The American Heritage Dictionary* speaks of *forgive* as, "to excuse for a fault or an offense; pardon; to renounce anger or resentment against; to refrain from imposing punishment on an offender or demanding satisfaction for an offense."

God may have to do special surgery on our hearts in this process, but I want all that He has for me. I want everything. The Bible tells us in Luke 6:37, "Judge not, and ye shall not be judged: condemn not, and ye shall not be condemned: forgive, and ye shall be forgiven:" In the original, forgive means: to set free, to release, to put away, to let go, to dismiss, to detain no longer (Strong's lexicon). Again let me emphasize that we do not have the power to accomplish this with our own human ability. We need His agape love shed abroad in our hearts to accomplish this. Let's cover this.

There are three dimensions of love that we can live in. These three dimensions come from actual Greek words. The first dimension, *phileo*, is friendship love. It's what you do when you seek to become friendly with someone, to have a friend. The Bible says for a man to have friends he must first be friendly (Proverbs

18:24.) Kind of like the concept of drawing more flies with honey than with vinegar.

The second dimension of love, *eros*, is romantic love between husbands and wives. The third word is *agape*.

Phileo and *eros* were the only "love" words in the original classic Greek. But *agape*, which is God's unending love or love without a motive or an agenda, was first introduced by Jesus. You cannot find the word *agape* in any original classic Greek writings, nor can you find it among any Old Testament documents.

Agape, God's Love

When Jesus introduced agape, it was so seldom used that it was not specific in its meaning. Therefore, our understanding of this word is based on how the Scriptures explain or use it. In Romans 12:9, it says, "Let love be without dissimulation. . . ." Dissimulation means without motive or without any strings attached.

In the three dimensions of love, you find that *agape* is the only love that God can empower us with. We have the human ability to have *phileo* love. We have the human ability to have *eros* love. But it is *not* humanly possible to express *agape* love. You cannot *agape* love without God's ability coming into your life. I want you to grasp that right now before I go any further. It's a very, very important building block for the area where we are headed.

Through your human ability you may learn how to *phileo* love. You can learn how to *eros* love by studying, reading, and practicing romance and applying this in a marriage. But *agape* love comes from God. And we're going to learn that God asks of us things that we are not humanly able to do. His grace enables us to perform any commandment He gives us.

We desire and need agape love poured into our hearts. If we pray in faith, He'll pour His agape love into us to empower us. The Bible says, "Now hope does not disappoint, because the love of God has been poured out in our hearts by the Holy Spirit . . ." (Romans 5:5 *NKJV*).

I've covered the three dimensions of love quickly, and we're going to slow down and cover them more specifically. I want to put these building blocks before you so that you can receive what God is wanting to impart to you.

These three dimensions of love are also found in Mark 12:29-31, "And Jesus answered him, The first of all the commandments is, Hear, O Israel; The Lord our God is one Lord: 30 And thou shalt love the Lord thy God with all thy heart, and with all thy soul, and with all thy mind, and with all thy strength: this is the first commandment. 31 And the second is like, namely this, Thou shalt love thy neighbour as thyself. *There is none other commandment greater than these."* (EMPHSIS MINE)

Jesus is simply reiterating the passage in Deuteronomy 6:5 except his time using the word "agape." Here is the first known instance of agape love being introduced. Here Jesus says, "And you shall agape the Lord your God." That's first. Love the Lord God "with all your heart, with all your soul, with all your mind, and with all your strength." This is the first commandment. And the second is like it: "You shall love your neighbor . . ." Number three: ". . . as yourself." Loving God, loving your neighbor, and loving yourself.

Notice what Jesus says next. There is no other commandment greater than these. Sometimes we put so much emphasis on things that don't even count in the eyes of God. Jesus said there's no other commandment greater than what? To love God, to love others, and to love yourself. You can have everything else together, you can have the entire Bible memorized, and be doing everything to a "T," but if there's not a love for God, a love for others, and a love for yourself, you've really not gained anything, you've actually missed it all. Everything begins with our drawing near to God and becoming intimate with Him so He can instill His agape love into our innermost heart of hearts. James 4:8 records, "Come close to God and He will come close to you. [Recognize that you are] sinners, get your soiled hands clean; [realize that you have been disloyal] wavering individuals with divided interests, and purify your hearts [of your spiritual adultery].ii

Notice, the degree we come to close to God is the degree He comes close to us. My passion for Him can determine the amount of His presence and power in my life. Now back to the commandment Jesus gave.

In this commandment we find the three fundamental relationships of life on which everything hangs. Jesus said that on *this* commandment hang all the law, the Old Testament, and the prophets. Everything hangs on our passionately loving God and drawing near to Him. Every principle the word of God contains is dependent on our intimacy with Him. This is an important building block in breaking the chains of shame in your life. I'm going to address some areas that I know you may find uncomfortable. Why? Because I'm going to deal with some areas that will have some past hurts and pain. These may include people who disappointed you, perhaps someone who abused you, molested you, or hurt you. Perhaps it's a situation that you don't want to have brought up again. You see, God doesn't want to leave that thing as it is. He wants to heal your heart. Why? So His love can pour forth from you, so His power and glory can be seen in you, so you can be all that God wants you to be.

A common deception of the enemy can be found in a phrase we have repeated somewhere in our lives. This phrase is "All things heal with time." This could never be more false. If all things healed simply with time passing by, then why have I sat in my office for hours, counseling 48 and 57 year old women who are still trying to sort through the emotional pain of a dad who went AWOL during her childhood or a abuse that occurred in her teens? The truth is, healing is a result of a disciplined decision, empowered by the Holy Spirit to forgive, release and forget offenses.

Loving God First

First, love the Lord your God. When we have unforgiveness towards God, it shows itself in rebellion. People who refuse to submit to authority just kind of wander from church to church, leadership covering to leadership covering. They are their own authority. The root of this rebellion is unforgiveness toward God. They never develop a truly intimate walk with God because somewhere in their hearts they blame God, even though their situation in life is a result of poor choices. The feel that somehow God did them wrong they.

This might have been what drove Moses out into the desert, away from the presence of God to simply keep sheep. The beauty is after 40 years wandering on the backside of the desert with those sheep, God dd not forget Moses. There came a day when God called for Moses to "turn aside". Anytime the Lord calls us to "turn aside", it is never convenient time. We're always "busy". There are times God calls me to prayer while I am sitting with friends or family. I have to make a decision. Do I want acceptance with people over intimacy with God. Some of the greatest supernatural experiences I have had with God happened when I chose to lay my busy schedule aside and seek His face. David said in Psalms 27:8, "When thou saidst, Seek ye my face; my heart said unto thee, Thy face, Lord, will I seek." The amazing truth in Exodus when God manifested His Theophany through a burning bush *was He did not speak to Moses until he had turned aside.* Exodus 3:3-4, "And Moses said, I will now turn aside, and see this great sight, why the bush is not burnt.

4 And when the Lord saw that he turned aside to see, God called unto him out of the midst of the bush, and said, Moses, Moses. And he said, Here am I." If Moses had felt he was too "busy" keeping the

flocks to take time to "turn aside" it is possible God would have left him alone and found another willing vessel. We can never get too busy "tending the Kingdom of God" that we do not daily take time to seek His face and listen to His voice.

Let me tell you something. Jesus will never do you wrong. Jesus will never fail you. He can do nothing but good. Man will fail you, "for offenses will come" but Jesus will *never* fail you! When someone harbors unforgiveness towards God and doesn't develop a intimate walk of love with God, it opens the door allowing rebellion to step through the doorway. They then live their lives completely for themselves with no desire to serve the King of Kings.

Here are some statements made by those who harbor unforgiveness towards God:

"I don't need the church to go to heaven!"

"I don't need a pastor!"

"It doesn't matter what God says, I'll live my life as I please!"

Those who harbor a grudge against God live lives of lawlessness.

You see, that's the original sin. That's why God hates it so much. The Bible says rebellion is as the sin of witchcraft (1 Samuel 15:23.) Satan desired to be like

God, but God says you can't, you're a created being. So Satan rose up in pride against God and in rebellion. Perhaps he felt that God had done him an injustice. He was cast out of heaven, and he's lived in rebellion ever since.

Satan was cast down from heaven to Earth and used to have power with God. I believe he had a close relationship as he was one of the three chief angels of God. The Bible says he walked amongst the stones of fire; he was closely acquainted with God's glory. But, because of the relationship with God becoming severed, rebellion filled his heart, and he said in Isaiah, "I will!" Isa 14:13-15, "For thou hast said in thine heart, I will ascend into heaven, I will exalt my throne above the stars of God: I will sit also upon the mount of the congregation, in the sides of the north:14 I will ascend above the heights of the clouds; I will be like the most High.15 Yet thou shalt be brought down to hell, to the sides of the pit."

Rebellion says, "I don't care what the Bible says! I'll do what I want to do! I don't care what the pastor says, I'll live my life my way!" I will wear what I what. I will go anywhere I want to. I will watch and listen to whatever I please. I will raise my children anyway I please. I will, I will, I will! Then you blame the church and the pastor when things go wrong and fall apart.

Somehow they become responsible for the fruit of your life of rebellion.

You see, in all probability it's *not* the pastor, it's not the church, my friend. Somewhere in your heart you've harbored unforgiveness towards God, and God is wooing you and drawing you that He might heal that rebellion in your spirit. The fruit of destruction n your life is the result of rebellion. Jesus died so you might live. Choose life today and choose the freedom of forgiveness.

You'll notice Jesus said to love the Lord with all your heart. He did not say to "serve the Lord." Why? He was talking to the Jews who had the "serving" part down. Serving God dutifully without having an intimate relationship with Him produces legalism. You can humanly serve God with all your heart, but you cannot *love* Him without the empowerment of agape! Jesus is asking us to do something that we humanly cannot do. Impossible! You can't within yourself serve God with all your heart.

The Jews understood what it was to serve, but Jesus threw them a curve and said, "Love the Lord." The love He is speaking about is not *phileo*, not *eros*, it's *agape*! When we rest in the truth that we are sons and daughters of God and rest in His love, then serving with all our hearts will be a natural outflow of our relationship with Him. We can do nothing to "qualify" or earn our Fathers love. Romans 5:8-9 records, "But God shows and clearly proves His [own] love for us by the fact that while we were still sinners, Christ (the Messiah, the Anointed One) died for us. 9 Therefore, since we are now justified (acquitted, made righteous, and brought into right relationship with God) by Christ's blood, how much more [certain is it that] we shall be saved by Him from the indignation and wrath of God."[iii] We are not justified by our own works but thru His blood.

If we do not receive this revelation then we will continually seek our identity by performance. Our identity is simply as sons and daughters of God! He was setting the stage with the power of His Spirit to fill the lives of mankind, to teach man once and for all how to be led by the Spirit of God. It cannot be by our own human ability or by being able to pull our own selves up by our boot straps. "God," we say, "I want You to love me." His reply? "But you're not going to love Me like I want you to love Me. The only way you can love Me is to let Me love *through* you."

It's God's love, not my love! Jesus coined this word "agape." Our love for God is not enough. We must agape the Lord with His love. Then really it is not my effort it is resting in His love. I don't have to fast for 21 days or pray for 14 hours straight to finally cleanse myself to the point that I can love him. I simply rest in His love, empowered by that love. Then I can fast 21 days and spend 14 hours in intimacy, communing and listening to his voice. All glory goes to Him! When I try to love Him within myself, I fail and get discouraged, or I'm depressed and not content. I can't love God like I want to love Him. It's not possible. But when I open my heart to him and say, "Pour your love through me! Jesus, love me! Let me love you with your love!"

Oh, that's when God can do the supernatural! That's when He can lift you into a dimension of love that you've never known! This is what Paul spoke of in Galatians 5:6, "For in Jesus Christ neither circumcision availeth anything, nor uncircumcision; but faith which worketh by love."

This kind of faith which worketh by love will see the blind eyes opened, deaf ears opened, the lame walk, the dead raised and the gospel preached to the millions.! This faith does not depend on my having just fasted a length of time or prayed all night or anything else. This faith is simply an overflow of the love of God in my heart resulting from my daily intimate walk with Him. The Greek word for *worketh* in this verse is;

energeo (en-erg-eh'-o); from NT:1756; to be active, effi-
cient: KJV - do, (be) effectual (fervent), be mighty in,
shew forthself, work (effectually in).[iv]

Jesus wants you to love Him with His love! Let
him!

The *phileo* love for our neighbor is not enough!
We must *agape*, agape our neighbor with His love.
We'll never love ourselves properly. Most people hate
themselves! We must agape ourselves with His love.
God wants to heal you!

Loving Your Neighbor

Love your neighbor. When we harbor unforgiveness toward our brother or sister, this produces bitterness. Bitterness in our hearts works like an acid. It
eats away the joy. It takes away the liberty and victory
in our lives. Nothing anyone ever could do against us
is worth holding onto and losing the peace of God in
our lives.

Did you ever notice how hard it is to worship
God freely when you're harboring unforgiveness
against your brother who sitting on the other side of
the church, worshipping God? All you can do is sit
there and say, "That hypocrite! Bless God! Why's she
up there singing? Why's he over there worshiping?
Who does he think he is?" While that person is singing

or worshiping, they have your victory right in their pocket, and you're letting it happen by harboring unforgiveness, and that bitterness will eat at you.

You know how I can tell that someone's harboring unforgiveness? It doesn't take very long being around them until the poison starts rolling out. You talk to them for a few minutes about the weather and, all of a sudden, poison starts coming forth. How do I know about this? A clue to myself that I am truly forgiving and releasing someone who has wronged me, is when I cease to discuss it at all. I simply turn it over to the Lord. God will even allow someone to bring their name up in conversation or even repeat a derogatory statement they might have said to test my spirit. If I say, "Yes, I love so-and-so and they are a good person, but... let me tell you what they did." I haven't forgiven. Some people bury the "hatchet" but they carefully mark the spot where it was buried. You have to let it die. Nothing is truly dead until it is buried. Oftentimes, I am the one who has to "die to my flesh" before an offense can truly die and be buried.

You can convince yourself, "Oh, I've forgiven that brother. I've forgiven that preacher. I've forgiven that person." But it's just words. The hurts are still there. If it still hurts, it means that God hasn't healed it. True healing and restoration cannot begin until I first choose to forgive and let it go.

I have a scar on my finger from when I was a teenager. I was working for a woodworking company and I got my finger caught in a belt sander. It pulled the tendons out. It was in a cast for about six months. For a year it was tender and painful. Now I can knock it against something and it's fine. Why? It's healed! If my finger was not healed and you grabbed my hand to shake it, I promise you that if it wasn't healed there would be serious pain! Then I would attack you and say, "you hurt me" even though you had no idea that area was tender. Some will say, "Oh, I've forgiven him." But the pain is still there – it is not healed. When you reach out to help then they attack you and accuse you of hurting them further, when all you tried to do was help them. You are not the problem; it is the bitterness in their spirit preventing the wound from healing.

I know when I have forgiven someone when I don't think about it anymore. I can go months and not think about it. That's how you know you've forgiven. Then God lets someone else hurt me and I have to work through it all over again. There must be something in my spirit that God's trying to purify. Sometimes I wish I could just crawl into a cave and not have contact with people. That way I don't have to worry about any more hurting/forgiveness scenarios. However, then I would never become promoted in His Kingdom. Promotion comes through the fire! When God allows an enemy to hurt you, get ready, He is about to promote you. A lot of enemies, then a BIG promotion is coming! When you have gotten past the pain and wiped your tears away, start rejoicing and dancing. The enemy did you a big favor trying to wound you because, the glory of God is about to be revealed.

When you've wept all night, when you've wept until you can't cry anymore, when you've gone through so much pain nobody knows what you feel except Jesus – that's when the bitterness tries to take root. Get up! Get up and begin praying blessing on those that hurt you. Jesus said in Matthew 5:44, "But I say unto you, Love your enemies, bless them that curse you, do good to them that hate you, and pray for them which despitefully use you, and persecute you;"

I make myself pray for that person no matter how hard the words are to say, "God bless them! God strengthen them!" I have to forgive them! I must! I may not feel like they deserve it but I will not give the advantage to the enemy! Furthermore, Jesus has forgiven me so much, I need to look daily for people to forgive.

As hard as the words are to come out, "God honor them, honor that person!"

Loving Ourselves

Love yourself. I am not talking about an unhealthy narcissism, but rather accepting His love and resting in the fact that I am a chosen son of God. When we harbor unforgiveness towards God, it is rebellion. When we harbor unforgiveness towards our neighbor, it is bitterness. When we refuse to release and forgive ourselves, we contend with guilt and shame.

Unresolved shame is one of the most debilitating spiritual conditions with which we contend today. Shame is unforgiveness toward ourselves. We hold ourselves emotionally hostage with regret about things we should not or should have done. Shame causes a person to feel like they will never accomplish anything in the Kingdom of God because of failures of the past. We must allow God to agape love even our own selves. We must allow His agape love to love Him through us, to love our neighbors through us, and to love ourselves through us. It is His agape love that enables us to accomplish this.

Why must I forgive? Why can't I just wish that person would slip and break his neck? Or just simply pray and ask God to zap them with a little bit of fire.

Why can't I wish just a little bit of ill or a little bit of badness towards that person that hurt me?

King David even dealt with his desire for revenge as recorded in Psalms 55:12-15, "For it was not an enemy that reproached me; then I could have borne it: neither was it he that hated me that did magnify himself against me; then I would have hid myself from him: 13 But it was thou, a man mine equal, my guide, and mine acquaintance. 14 We took sweet counsel together, and walked unto the house of God in company. 15 Let death seize upon them, and let them go down quick into hell: for wickedness is in their dwellings, and among them."

I'm going to tell you why according to the Bible: as I mentioned before, unforgiveness gives the enemy the advantage.

You see, when you're fighting for revival, when you're fighting for souls, you need every advantage you can get, but when you choose not to forgive, you give the enemy advantage in your life.

Paul said, "Now whom you forgive anything, I also forgive" (II Corinthians 2:10 *NKJV*). Paul wanted to forgive everybody. That's how we need to be. Furthermore, he said, "I have forgiven them . . . lest Satan should take advantage of us; for we are not ignorant of his devices" (2:10-11). He's talking about forgiving. He said, "If I don't forgive, Satan will take advantage of us." Paul understood Satan's weapons. Many good children of God that live good clean lives thwart their own success because they harbor unforgiveness and are giving the devil an advantage.

We cannot truly deal with forgiving ourselves or loving ourselves until we first forgive others. Peter came to Jesus asking, "Lord, how often shall my brother sin against me, and I forgive him? Up to seven times?" Matthew 18:21^v

Peter was being very generous. According to the rabbinic teachings, the offended party only had to forgive his brother three times – that's it! So Peter was saying, "Well, let me double that and add one on top for good measure. I'm pretty righteous, Lord . . . seven times?"

Jesus said, "I do not say to you, up to seven times, but up to seventy times seven" (18:22). He was basically saying don't set a limit on it, my friend. At any rate, forgiving someone 490 times in one day for an offense is quite a task! Every time you forgive, you become empowered against the devil. When you don't forgive, the enemy gets the advantage against you.

You might ask, "Why, God? I'm over here trying to do a good work, and someone lies about me and slanders me. They accuse me of immoral conduct. Why, God? They've lied about my family and said hurtful words against my wife, and . . . WHY?" Well, to be used of God we have to pas the hurt test. If we can be lied on, slandered, cheated etc... and not get bitter then, we can truly be used greatly by the Lord. Jesus knows any time in life that people wrong you and you choose to forgive from the heart – not just with words. When you choose to release it, to not talk about it, to not dwell on it, then you become empowered!

Now here is how Jesus answered Peter's question:

23."Therefore the kingdom of heaven is like a certain king who wanted to settle accounts with his servants. 24.And when he had begun to settle accounts, one was brought to him who owed him ten thousand talents. 25.But as he was not able to pay, his master commanded that he be sold, with his wife and children and all that he had, and that payment be made. 26.The servant therefore fell down before him, saying, 'Master, have patience with me, and I will pay you all.' 27.Then the master of that servant was moved with compassion, released him, and forgave him the debt.

28."But that servant went out and found one of his fellow servants who owed him a hundred denarii; and he laid hands on him and took *him* by the throat, saying, 'Pay me what you owe!' 29·So his fellow servant fell down at his feet and begged him, saying, 'Have patience with me, and I will pay you all.' 30·And he would not, but went and threw him into prison till he should pay the debt.

31."So when his fellow servants saw what had been done, they were very grieved, and came and told their master all that had been done. 32·Then his master, after he had called him, said to him, 'You wicked servant! I forgave you all that debt because you begged me. 33·Should you not also have had compassion on your fellow servant, just as I had pity on you?' 34·And his master was angry, and **delivered him to the torturers** until he should pay all that was due to him.

35."So My heavenly Father also will do to you if each of you, **from his heart**, does not forgive his brother his trespasses" (Matthew 18:23-35, *NKJV,* emphasis added).

This servant owed ten thousand talents – a talent was eighty pounds of gold – millions of dollars.

The king ordered that the man's wife, children, and possessions be sold to pay his debt. But then, because he asked him, the king canceled the debt. No compromise. No installment plan. No ninety-days-same-as-cash. He canceled it. He struck it off the books!

I remember the day I came to my King – my debt was so great. I owed such a liability that there was no way to pay. I was carrying the weight of sin from Adam to my father and my own sins. Could I pay it? No, but God forgave me.

Instead of this servant going forth and mirroring what his master did, he found a servant owing a hundred denarii. That money is valued at about three month's wages. This was not a frivolous amount. Often we are willing to forgive and let go of small things in life but somewhere we draw he line and expect re-payment or apologies. This "drawing the line" is what gets us in trouble. I have forgiven people of small amounts but when the amount being stolen became over $60,000 then I decided to draw a line in the sand. This cost me dearly in the spirit (I will tell this account a little later in this chapter.) To demand re-payment and take a brother to court is a form of un-forgiveness. The servant demanded payment. Hearing about it, the king sent him to the tormentors.

Notice this – the king had forgiven the man his debt. It was gone. But, because he chose not to forgive the other one his debt that in comparison was so insignificant, the king reversed what he'd already done and sent him to the place of torment.

Could it be that sometimes we struggle against past faults and flaws that we thought we'd overcome? Could it be that we take ourselves out from under the covering of His blood and blessings by choosing to not forgive? Could it be that God, who is so merciful to us, who has forgiven all that, when we choose not to forgive, could remove that covering of blood?

Jesus also said that we are not to offer our gift on the altar until we have reconciled with our brother whom we have aught against. Reconciliation and forgiveness are not something I was taught growing up. God is teaching me that reconciliation and forgiveness should be the goal of our walk with God. When a greatly used Minister in Africa who has seen over 2 million filed with the Spirit, preaches to the church he is leading, he does not preach revival. He preaches unity. He preaches reconciliation and loving your brother, forgiving and releasing. Why don't I want to release my brother? Because, if I do, he's off the hook, and he won't have to pay for what he did to me. That's why I harbor that anger. That's why I keep that bitterness.

Recently I was struggling with a major test in my life. (I mentioned this earlier). I was struggling with a debt that was owed to me of over $60,000. I would setle it in prayer and give it to the Lord but, then someone would come along that had heard about this situation and start saying, " You are not being done right." "You need to do something about this." "Think about your family, this is food, clothes and shelter for them." Then I would get upset all over again and stew over the situation. I knew the Spirit had instructed me to release this situation into His hands, but I kept allowing myself to get stirred up. Finally after receiving a disappointing letter from this party, I decided to file charges against them. I gathered all the copies of proof for the debt and sent it with a letter filing the charges. I was leaving that day to China to minister in a leadership conference. I felt good about what I did for about 30 minutes of the drive to the airport. Then the Lord began to gently rebuke me. He asked, "Son, did I not command you to release this to me?" I replied with all the ways we were being done unjustly. The gentle rebuke of the Lord simply continued into the flight to China and up till I checked into my hotel. That night I could not sleep. Every person that had hurt me or my wife in the past 9 years of pasturing, their faces came before me. I could see their snarls of hate and bitterness. I rose out of bed and began to pace the floor fervently praying in the spirit to no avail. I finally collapsed in bed from exhaustion and slept a few hours. After 8 hours of teaching the next day to the leaders, I once again went to my hotel to get caught up on my sleep only to have the same scenes flash before my face. At about 3 am I fell on my face crying out to God saying, "Lord, what is going on? How come I do not have the authority to bind these attacks in prayer? I am desperate, I need to sleep." Then the Lord quietly replied, "My son, when you sent that letter to force repayment of the debt, that was a form of unforgiveness. I have forgiven you a great debt however; your demands for repayment have caused the tormentors of all your past hurts to return." I immediately fell on my face in contrite repentance, then rose and typed a letter releasing the charge I had filed. I left the room and faxed the letter from China. That night I slept like a baby. Again I say, no offense in this life is worth losing your peace of God over.

We must forgive. We know when we've forgiven, because we've forgotten. Genesis 37-41, Joseph goes through all kinds of injustice. His brothers sell him into slavery. He is lied on and cheated, his character slandered but he forgave. Genesis 41:51-52 records,

"And Joseph called the name of the firstborn Manasseh: For God, said he, hath made me forget all my toil, and all my father's house.52 And the name of the second called he Ephraim: For God hath caused me to be fruitful in the land of my affliction."

Manasseh is derived from the Hebrew word Menashsheh (men-ash-sheh'); from OT:5382; which means -*causing to forget*;[vi] (EMPHASIS MINE)

Ephraim is derived from the Hebrew word Ephrayim (ef-rah'-yim); which means dual of masculine form of OT:672; *double fruit*;[vii] (EMPHASIS MINE)

The reason God finally lifted him to the place He had promised him, causing him to become doubly fruitful, was because he chose to forgive and forget. God had said the sun, stars, and moon would bow down. He held onto that promise from God, but, in the meantime, he went through a trial of fire that could have made him bitter. Joseph chose to forgive and forget. Why do I know he chose to forgive? Because the Bible says Joseph called the name of his firstborn son "Manasseh." Manasseh means "causing to forget." Joseph could have remained in Potiphar's household forever, I believe, if he had chosen not to forgive. But, because he chose to forgive, God honored and blessed him in a double manner. Some people say, "I'll forgive, but, bless God, I'm not going to forget! I'll forgive, but you give me a chance and I'll tell everyone in the world about it."

Joseph overcame his fiery trial because he did not take the attacks of his brethren or Potiphar's wife personal. He understood that promotion come from the fire! This is why Joseph could say in Genesis 45:4-5, "And Joseph said unto his brethren, Come near to me, I pray you. And they came near. And he said, I am Joseph your brother, whom ye sold into Egypt.

5 Now therefore be not grieved, nor angry with yourselves, that ye sold me hither: for God did send me before you to preserve life."

Also in Genesis 50:20, "But as for you, ye thought evil against me; but God meant it unto good, to bring to pass, as it is this day, to save much people alive."

Peter spoke of the trial by fire in which every chosen child of God must face to purify and develop His purpose in their lives in 1 Peter 4:12-13, "Beloved, think it not strange concerning the fiery trial which is to try you, as though some strange thing happened unto you:13 But rejoice, inasmuch as ye are partakers of Christ's sufferings; that, when his glory shall be revealed, ye may be glad also with exceeding joy."

The trial of fire is not there to destroy us but rather to develop us. Fire is a purification and refining agent. When you heat water to about 212 degrees Fahrenheit at sea level, then water will begin to boil. At roughly 400 degrees Fahrenheit, wood will begin to burn. At 900 degrees Fahrenheit, iron will begin to melt. However, gold does not begin to melt until 2200 degrees Fahrenheit. God will use the wounds we receive in the houses of our friends to develop us into pure Holy Ghost gold if we will not take things personally and recognize His purpose is being fulfilled through what the enemy or people intended to destroy us. Don't be a bowl of water that, "poof" evaporates the moment the heat is on, but take your wounds to the foot of the cross and let His Spirit and blood do a supernatural work that only He can do!

Endnotes

---

[i] AMP

[ii] Ibid

[iii] Ibid

[iv] Biblesoft's New Exhaustive Strong's Numbers and Concordance with Expanded Greek-Hebrew Dictionary. Copyright © 1994, 2003, 2006 Biblesoft, Inc. and International Bible Translators, Inc.

[v] *NKJV*

[vi] Biblesoft's New Exhaustive Strong's Numbers and Concordance with Expanded Greek-Hebrew Dictionary. Copyright © 1994, 2003, 2006 Biblesoft, Inc. and International Bible Translators, Inc.

[vii] Ibid

2
The Shame Game

The concept of self-forgiveness has revelatory power and has released untold numbers of people from shame, guilt, and self-loathing – wilderness times. There are times when God sends us into the wilderness because He wants to reveal to us not only who He is, but who we are. Every man or woman whom God has ever used had to go through a wilderness time. Everyone who has gone through a wilderness time, God is calling them to reveal His power and Glory!

David said in Psalm 63:1-2, 1."O God, thou *art* my God; early will I seek thee: my soul thirsteth for thee, my flesh longeth for thee in a dry and thirsty land, where no water is; 2.To see thy power and thy glory, so *as* I have seen thee in the sanctuary."

I believe that God is calling the church as a unit to a place of deeper inner healing and a greater revelation of our desperate need for intimacy with Him. I travel all over the world and I and surprised by the count-less people, ministry and saints alike, that have no clue what a truly intimate relationship with God is all about. They are familiar with organization, structure and the fellowship of the saints, but do not passionate-ly seek a deeper relationship with the Lord. Sad to say, I preach in conferences and churches where the pastor or leader in charge of the conference has no clue when God shows up. He or she just continues on with their set program, oblivious the King of Kings has just showed up to do a mighty work. Any good that has come through my ministry owes its credit to the inner healing of God's Spirit and revelation of my desperate need for greater intimacy with Him. Lately, I find my-self weeping on airplanes, in hotel rooms, hungry for a closer walk with Him. I feel the cry of Moses, "shew me thy glory." Unfortunately many are like Aaron, who was more comfortable in the fellowship of people than in the presence of the glory of God. His desire to please men and not God was one of the reasons the golden calf was produced. When God marks us to seek His face, we need to earnestly seek His face.

In your life, my friend, there exists some mark, some fiber of the Holy Ghost that has been put into you that God wants to draw out in the beauty of His power and grace and love. This comes by the power of inner healing, and so we become released in the spirit realm. It is not just an individual work; God is at work in the church body as a whole. He wants to release the beauty and the power of His Spirit.

The Forgiveness Factor – Unlocking the Chains of Shame

The American Heritage Dictionary speaks of *forgive* as, "to excuse for a fault or an offense; pardon; to renounce anger or resentment against; to refrain from imposing punishment on an offender or demanding satisfaction for an offense." As I mentioned in chapter one, there are three areas of unforgiveness. First, unforgiveness towards God brings rebellion. It is amazing how many people harbor such feelings against Him. Often they don't even realize they have these feelings because that is how deception works – you don't even know you're deceived. So their unforgiveness towards God causes them to "hold God hostage" or to hold a grudge against Him for situations in their life. This ends in rebellion towards Him. I can often sense when someone has unforgiveness towards God because they refuse to submit themselves to any form of authority whatsoever; they won't submit to God's Word. What they need desperately is healing in their lives to get over it.

When we harbor unforgiveness toward our brother or sister, it produces bitterness. We discussed that in the parable of unforgiveness. There are dangers of harboring bitterness – that acid that takes our joy away. It puts poison in a person's spirit making him unkind, vindictive, and generally unpleasant to be around.

Finally, when we refuse to forgive and release ourselves, we contend with shame and guilt. Unresolved shame is one of the most debilitating spiritual conditions we contend with in this hour. We must allow God to *agape* love Him through us, love our neighbors through us, and to love ourselves through us.

This second principle about forgiving ourselves is not something we can do in our own power. It takes a supernatural healing and empowerment work of God's Spirit. It takes God's love through us to love our enemies – to love those who mistreat us and spitefully use us. Our human reaction is to get even – to not love. If we depend on our human *phileo* and *eros* types of love, we will fall woefully short. Becoming available to the love of God, which the Word of God says "is shed abroad in our hearts by the Holy Ghost" (Romans 5:5), then through the power of God's love, the amazing principle of God loving through us, we can love.

This is what we must understand – it is the miracle power of God that allows us to love in ways that we could not otherwise. It is not us loving; it is God loving through us. We've got to understand this so that, when we've come through the storm, when we're on the other side of the pain of a situation, and when we've become healed and have truly forgiven, we will then understand that it was not within ourselves to accomplish this. It comes simply through faith in prayer. I pray often, "God, see if there is any unforgiveness in my heart toward any situation, any person, or anything and, if there is, ignite my heart with Your love. By faith I believe you can flow your love through me toward any person." The Bible says that "love will cover a multitude of sins" (I Peter 4:8 *NKJV*). He can do it through us.

As we go through these principles, you will experience something more life-transforming than many exciting "shoutin' services" you've ever been to in your life. This may be more life-transforming than anything you've ever come across. Why? Because I know – I have experienced it changing and transforming my life, too! And I put my pants on one leg at time like anyone else – I'm not a super-spiritual creature. I know if God can help me, then He can help others.

Forgive yourself. Luke 6:37 says, "Judge not, and ye shall not be judged: condemn not, and ye shall not be condemned: forgive, and ye shall be forgiven:" Remember, "forgive" means to set free, to release, to let go, to dismiss. Let us understand what it means to forgive – we must forgive and forget. God forgives and forgets:

Psalms 103:8-12, [8.]"The LORD *is* merciful and gracious, slow to anger, and plenteous in mercy. [9.]He will not always chide: neither will he keep *his anger* for ever. [10.]He hath not dealt with us after our sins; nor rewarded us according to our iniquities. [11.]For as the heaven is high above the earth, *so* great is his mercy toward them that fear him. [12.]As far as the east is from the west, *so* far hath he removed our transgressions from us."

Notice the distinction here between the words "sin" and "iniquity." Sin is a mistake. Sin is a flaw. Iniquity is self-will and rebellion against God. But God knows how to deal with both by the power of His blood and by the power of His Spirit.

Claim it right now – "I'm forgiven." Many times we pray about things that God doesn't even recall. You are living your life trying to serve God and, all of a sudden, you blow it, you mess up, you do something

46

stupid. You then fall before God and seek His face; He comes to you with His love and draws you, washes you, and forgives you. He then empowers you to overcome that thing. Many people come back to God days later and bring back up the shame and the guilt because they have not forgiven themselves. So they draw it back up again, but God says, "I don't know what you're talking about – you're wasting your breath!" You cannot reach beneath the blood to dredge back sins that have already been covered. They're gone forever. He's wiped the slate clean. He's thrown them in the sea of His forgetfulness and puts up a giant sign that says "No Fishing."

Accepting Forgiveness

You've got to understand and accept by faith "He's forgiven me!" Then you can forgive yourself. The burden of shame and guilt can be so heavy. We cannot truly love God and others until we have loved, forgiven, and released ourselves. Many people don't understand why they can't love their husband or wife or their children or neighbor – usually it is because of unresolved guilt and shame within themselves. Unforgiveness can be compared to wounds that never heal.

Let me give you a little illustration of what it can do. According to an article I found in Readers Digest,

April 1991 issue, about a redwood tree that suffered a wound from which it did not recover.

In the early morning hours of the thirteenth of March 1933, a tall, majestic redwood tree suddenly came crashing to the ground. After a careful examination of a cross-section of the tree and a count of the growth rings, California forestry experts declared that a life of more than twelve centuries had come to an end. Through the science of tree chronology, they were able to piece together the history of this once mighty redwood. According to their analysis, the tree had experienced both periods of fatness and leanness – sometimes experiencing times of rapid growth and other times near stagnation. In one cross-section, one hundred and twelve rings occupied only eight inches. The next hundred rings occupied thirty-six inches. In 1147, a "ring-shake," or possibly an earthquake, had left stringy wind-rot in the crevice, and the tree had been strong, and the rot had been defeated. In 1595 when Shakespeare was a young traveling player, the tree suffered a serious burn, which allowed fungus to grow beneath the bark. But the tree overcame the effects of the burn with new bark, and the fungus eventually died off.

For nearly two hundred years thereafter, the tree grew in peace. Then, because of lightning strikes and Indian fires, the tree again faced threats to is existence. A serious burn occurred in 1787 and another in 1806. The worst occurred in 1820 leaving a thirteen-foot scar. During this fire, the roots on the north side of the tree were burned away, and slowly the tree began to lean. At the time of the 1820 burn, this beautiful redwood was at its prime, three hundred and twenty feet tall and weighing over five hundred tons. For over a century it struggled to overcome the effects of this tragic event, but, in the end, the wound never fully healed, and the tree ultimately was forced to yield to its weakening forces. And so it was on the morning of that late winter day, the tree finally reached the point of critical balance. Something, perhaps nothing more than a little bird landing on a limb, or perhaps a small gust of wind swirling against the branches, proved to be more than the tree could bear, and it toppled to the ground.

Many people have their rings of spiritual growth. We've all had our good times of exceptional personal growth and our bad times of growth. And we've had our times of stagnation spiritually. But how is it that someone who seemed to be so spiritually strong would suddenly one day fall to seemingly the slightest situation. It is wounds that didn't heal in that person's spirit – ashes of bitterness. One day they were such strong prayer warriors; shortly after, they left their walk with God. I've seen people that were so faithful to God's Word – people who gave themselves to God's kingdom, people who were so full of love. You meet them years later, and they've fallen and are so full of anger, resentment, and bitterness. You wonder what could have possibly taken someone that strong. What could have ever destroyed the faith of someone like that?

Proverbs 18:14 tells us, "The spirit of a man will sustain his infirmity; but a wounded spirit who can bear?"

A wounded spirit is too heavy for the human spirit to carry. Tall trees in the spirit realm do catch the full force of the wind. They do attract all kinds of resentments, petty jealousies, and hurtful attacks. Spiritual redwoods can be damaged by fires of mistrust and dishonesty, hurt and pain. None of us are immune to this. God has equipped us with the ability to weather these storms as long as healing occurs afterward.

To many people's view, the tree's demise may have been a surprise, but the tree knew all along that something wasn't right. So, we stand and shake our heads at a fallen brother or sister, yet they were not surprised – they knew they were eroded and burned-out spiritually. They knew they had lost their appetite for the things of the Spirit due to lack of intimacy with Him. We usually end up hungering for that which we feed upon. They thought they could fill the empty spaces of their spirit with entertainment or working hard for the kingdom. Something you thought you could just ignore – just worship over, just keep doing what you've always done, just keep coming to church, just keep singing the same songs, keep doing the same things – but somewhere inside something was eating at you. Something was taking way the joy and victory of your soul – it's the wound that never ever healed. There are some wounds that are so deep that the only way we can bear them is to take them to Jesus. God is drawn to those who in the depth of their pain and suffering, choose to become broken and seek His face in desperation. This is illustrated in Isaiah 66:2, "For all these things My hand has made, and so all these things have come into being [by and for Me], says the Lord. But this is the man to whom I will look and have regard: he who is humble and of a broken or wounded spirit, and who trembles at My word and reveres My commands." (AMP)

Offenses Will Come

Jesus said, "Offenses will come." We don't have to fear attacks by friends, we just need to fear the failure of healing and forgiveness. With a proper perspective of the fear of the Lord and love for Him, we can recover from the wounds life deals to us. Lack of healing and not forgiving destroys our spiritual strength. I have observed many saints jumping from one church to the next. During my travels, I will see them at one church and then at another the following year. Everywhere they go they have a story to tell. They had a bone to pick with someone. My heart goes out to those people – it's not the church, pastor, people, or even the standards of living, it's a festering wound that never was submitted to the power of the Holy Ghost to be healed.

Deep inside, a wound has crippled some people who still come to church, who still do what's expected, but my prayer is that the Holy Spirit of God will begin His healing restoration work in their spirit. Let the love of God take over and let Jesus forgive that person through you! Let Him rewrite your identity so that your past has no more dictates on your future. We don't need any more brothers and sisters to fall. We don't need to lose one more person! We have the power of His healing by His Spirit!

Shame and guilt destroy faith. I John 3:19-21 says, 19."And by this we know that we are of the truth, and shall assure our hearts before Him. 20.For if our heart condemns us, God is greater than our heart, and knows all things. 21.Beloved, if our heart does not condemn us, we have confidence toward God" (*NKJV*).

Shame robs us of that faith and confidence in God. Some people are constantly saying, "Oh, I hope that God can solve that. I hope God will do this for me." Why do they speak this way? Why is their faith so shallow. It is because shame has not been resolved in their spirit. They have not tapped into the "faith which worketh by love." Somewhere shame has never been healed and dealt with. Their confidence in God has been shaken. This is the main reason the enemy stirs those to attack and wound us. He is trying to strip us of our authority and shake our confidence in God operating the gift through us. This is why Jesus said to Peter in Luke 22:31-32, "And the Lord said, Simon, Simon, behold, Satan hath desired to have you, that he may *sift you as wheat*:32 But I have prayed for thee, that thy faith fail not: and when thou art converted, strengthen thy brethren." (EMPHASIS MINE)

Peter did not understand this "faith which works by love" until after Calvary. While Peter was counting fish, Jesus asked him, "Simeon, lovest thou me." (John 21:15-17) After the third time, Jesus asked Peter the question, he received the revelation agape love. This is what empowered him to preach to the multitudes who had just crucified Christ on the day of Pentecost and eventually willingly allow himself to be crucified upside down for preaching the Name of Jesus.

Faith in the New Testament is so much different than faith in the Old Testament. In the Old Testament it is mentioned twice. In the New Testament it is mentioned 229 times! In the original language, Old Testament faith meant "faithfulness, firmness, steadfastness, steadiness, or serving God." But in the New Testament, with the advent of the Law of the Spirit of Life that overcame the law of sin, faith became confidence, belief, assurance, and trust in Christ. Faith is simple. God does not answer complex faith. He answers faith that simply believes He will do what He said He would do. You see, He so wants the power of His love to empower us. You can be faithful, my friend. You can come to church every day the doors are open, every time the lights are on, but if you don't have faith in God, you won't go anywhere. You will stagnate. You'll die. Some people are barely serving God because they've got a strong will and are just determined to serve God. But it's mundane. It is a dead experience – it has no life. But that is not the will of God. God's will is life and life more abundantly – to know the passion and the intimacy of His presence, to know what it means to truly wake up in the morning trusting fully with confidence in God.

I don't want to just go through the motions. I don't want to just hang on until the rapture comes – God, fill my heart with faith! We cannot serve God effectively out of mere duty. We must serve Him with love and a passionate heart of faith. That's why the Lord wrote, ". . . I will put My law in their minds, and write it on their hearts; and I will be their God, and they shall be My people" (Jeremiah 31:33b, *NKJV*).

"So, what do I do, if I have shame that is robbing my faith and short-circuiting my confidence in God? What do I do?"

You can rise no higher than what your faith in God's ability will allow. If somehow you feel deep down inside that God cannot use you, then He will not. I've often said that God may want to do awesome things for people, but if we believe that God will go only so far then, even when God begins to open those doors in our lives, there is something in the human nature to abort it – to keep us from going into that dimension. I've seen it happen hundreds of times to people who had tremendous potential in God, but they could not believe God for what God wanted to accomplish for and through them. How do I unlock the kind of faith that will allow me to be used greatly buy the Lord? We unlock it through our daily passionate pursuit of His presence and favor. Moses probably should have had faith to take the world, but he could never conquer the shame of what happened in Egypt. Though he was a great leader with great ability, he could never truly lead God's people fully into all the promises. You see, I don't want anything to hold me back any more than I want anyone else to be kept from attaining all that God has for them in every area and every promise.

Moses was so tied to the shame and the guilt of his failure back in Egypt that, when God wanted to wipe out the children of Israel, the first thing that came to Moses' mind was "what will the Egyptians think?"(Numbers 14:12-14) Moses could not believe God to use him to lead a group of young people into Canaan and take the land. Instead he chose to remain with the rebellious, murmuring people that had left Egypt but Egypt had not left their heart. This eventually resulted in his breaking in anger and smiting the rock when God told him to speak to the rock and finally being refused by God entry into the Promise Land. (Numbers 20:11-12)

Let God Love You

If I feel I am unlovable or unworthy of His love, I will refuse to let God love me and will also reject the love of others.

Due to past hurt and the resulting bitterness and rebellion, many people live with "walls" in their spirit. They make it as difficult as possible for someone to develop a relationship with them. It is as if they are saying, "I'll keep you so far at a distance you'll never break through all my resistances."

God cannot love us against our own will. God cannot love you against your will. You say, "Oh, But, God is love." Yes, He is. He also said, "Whosoever will." Have you ever tried to show love to someone against their will? It's not going to happen. The love of God never ends, but we can perceive to be unloved and live our lives in that manner as a result of shame.

Because of emotional and physical abuse that I had suffered, I struggled against this many times. Often times, the way we feel toward our own selves may not be the way God feels towards us, but perceived rejection and perceived lack of love is as real as actual rejection. Yes, God may love you, yes, your pastor may love you, but if you don't feel that God loves you, then that is where the real problem lies. In your life that is all that matters – it is your reality. If you perceive that somehow, because of unresolved shame, that a person rejects you, that is how it will appear to you regardless of reality. Anything perceived can be as real as something actual if healing doesn't take place.

Because of physical and emotional abuse I suffered from my parents, it has taken a very long time for me to be comfortable with anybody of any importance in my life – for me to be able to let them hug me. I can remember when my pastor would come up and hug me and I would push away. Everything within me wanted to receive love from Bro. Kilgore, but that unresolved shame had warped my reality. I needed healing because I didn't love myself. I rejected myself and expected everyone else to reject me. I didn't love myself, and I didn't expect anyone else to love me, especially God. I served God out of desire and commitment.

When it began to dawn on me how much He really loved me, the walls began to fall and healing began to take place. When I understood how much He yearns for us and longs for a close intimate walk with Him, then I began to draw nearer to him with an increased intensity. I began seeking His face and to know Him with a ferocious intensity. I began to melt in the reality of His love discovered through intimacy with Him. When we don't accept God's forgiveness and love because we feel unlovable or ashamed, then we are in essence unloved even though God loves us – His love never ends. We are unloved because we short-change ourselves. We live our lives as though God did not love us.

So many Christians who do not understand this truth try to earn the Father's love with service and performance. They find their identity in religious performance. Earthly fathers may try to make you earn their love, but our Heavenly Father will never! Gods' desire to draw us close and love us will always be greater than our desire to draw close to and love Him. God is daily just looking for someone to shine His favor and love upon. 2 Chronicles 16:9a records, "For the eyes of the Lord run to and fro throughout the whole earth to show Himself strong in behalf of those whose hearts are blameless toward Him." (AMP)

People live their lives as though God did not love them due to self-rejection. Because we don't forgive ourselves, we live with continual perceived rejection. I have experienced this. I would sit on the front row as a young man in Austin, Texas, and cry because I thought my pastor didn't like me. He was just a man who always looked intense and serious. However, my perceptions about authority figures was already being molded by the beginning abuses taking place in our home.

Did you know that you project your human spirit fifteen feet around you? When I see a person who is Spirit filled from a distance, often my spirit will go and greet them before I physically do. If you are broadcasting self-rejection because you've not forgiven and released yourself from some situation, people may not reject you, but you will perceive that they do because that is all that's around you. We can even invite unwanted emotional reactions by the spirit we project. We project a positive, wholesome faith filled spirit, the same is drawn to us. When we project negative worry, doubt, fear ect... the same can be drawn to us.

When I first entered the field of full-time evangelism, I would attend various church conferences. Sometimes I would be sitting there and look over at pastors talking and laughing and think they were making fun of me. If a pastor walked up and didn't shake my hand, I thought he hated me. Why? Because of the abuse, rejection, and pain I had gone through. Even though I wanted to serve God, I didn't like myself. I so severely rejected myself that every single interpersonal relationship in life was affected by it. Shame became the grudge against myself. Thank God I have been completely healed and delivered today!

What Is Shame?

What is shame? Where does it even come from? First, it's the painful feeling of loss of respect for ones self.

Secondly, it is the feeling of inadequacy or inferiority. I have experienced this many times in the past. You try to get in a group of people but just feel so inferior and unworthy of their company. Now I live daily in the peace and security of His love and approval. I walk daily in the love and fear of the Lord.

It is the feeling that esteem and respect is lost in the eyes of those of significance in our lives. It carries feelings of perceived or actual failure. Sometimes it shows up in our dreams. You might dream that you go to an important event with just your underwear on. We can hide it but, if it is not dealt with, it will surface somewhere in our lives. I used to dream that I was at General Conference preaching with only my underwear on. That's paralyzing!

The identity, the source of shame, can also be traced to interpersonal relationships with people of significance in our lives whom we wish to please or gain approval from. When we suffer rejection from someone we consider important, it often causes us to reject ourselves. Shame screams in your ear, "You're defective; you'll never be good enough. People will reject you when they find out who you really are." Let me tell you something, my friend, Jesus can transform the skeletons of shame in your life into the trophies of His grace if you'll let Him.

I want you to be delivered. I don't want anyone to suffer one day the things I've suffered. I want you to be transformed and to see you used by God to do ten times more than what I've done. I want to see chains released and the yokes broken! We are always going to face sources of shame. We will never escape it.

What do you do if life keeps hurting you? Face it! Those things don't go away; they will always be there through one means or another. It is not possible to extinguish every flame of hurt before it burns you; the answer is to stock a ready supply of the healing balm of forgiveness so that permanent damage is prevented. Learn to forgive the moment and offense is committed, before it can get down into your spirit and cause damage. Solomon admonished us in Proverbs 18:8, "The words of a talebearer are as wounds, and they go down into the innermost parts of the belly." We have to catch the wounding words and actions before they affect our spirit. Take them to the Lord and ask Him to help you forgive and release them.

Forgive God, others, and yourself by the love of God. Exercise it on a daily basis on a personal level through a passionate relationship with Jesus Christ. It doesn't matter how many fires are started when we discover that intimate relationship with God and that He loves us, period; He's forgiven us, period! Then we can forgive ourselves. The we live in the freedom of forgiveness, at peace, knowing we are loved and approved of God. That is all that matters. This is not some self-help, New Age idea. I'm talking about having the love of God shed abroad in our hearts. (See Romans 5:5.)

I'm approved of God. I'm accepted of God. I'm a child of God. It is supernatural healing. It's not getting up in the morning and looking yourself in the eye and saying, "You're something awesome, you're something awesome, you're something awesome." You can listen to every subliminal tape and ego booster, and they will do nothing for you like the power of God's love will to overcome shame. This love is only discovered when we feed the appetites of our spiritual man with the presence of God and things that please Him. The beauty is that you don't have to do anything extraordinary. You don't need to climb any rungs and go through qualification tests, just by faith release it to God in prayer. I challenge you when you pray to say, "I'm asking you, Lord, by the power of Your Spirit that resides in me, overcome shame, overcome guilt, overcome unresolved unforgiveness in my heart." He'll do it, my friend.

Other Sources of Shame

Shame sometimes comes from one's own actions such as sin, bad decisions, and living with regret, especially over sexual sins – fornication, adultery, homosexuality, etc. I'm talking to someone who is a victim of molestation or incest as a child or even a victim of rape. Shame is especially strong when these wounds are inflicted by someone trusted or loved. However, when God truly heals us, we don't live with regrets of our past, just memories. Some people live regretting the day they were born because of shame and hurt. But when Jesus really heals us, we don't live with regrets. We live with anticipation and faith, looking towards he life we have in Christ.

Sometimes shame comes from goals a person did not achieve, which may cause them to feel that their life is incomplete, or that it hasn't reached its fullest potential. Sometimes you may want to do so much good for God that, when you miss a good opportunity, shame will block your abilities for the rest of your life saying, "You missed it, you'll never be what you could have been. You'll never go where you could have gone." If you fast and pray and submit yourself to a good pastor, you will be in God's will for your life. God won't let you get out of His will if your heart is right before Him. The enemy will use our goals against us to try to cause condemnation. When we walk in the liberty of Christ, we can say with Paul in Romans 8:1, "There is therefore now no condemnation to them which are in Christ Jesus, who walk not after the flesh, but after the Spirit."

I remember in the fall of 2006, I felt the Lord call me on a 40 day fast. I fasted with mostly water and an occasional glass of grapefruit juice if I had to preach to give me a little strength. Once I crossed the 21st day, it was mainly water. I remember when I reached the 38th day god spoke to me and said, "Ok, my son, your finished now, break your fast." I spent the whole day struggling with this as I was determined to go the full 40 days. I finally gave in the morning of the 39th day and broke the fast with a bowl of tomato soup. Immediately I felt as though I was backslid. The enemy berated me and condemned me as though I was a vile sinner. I felt as though I had failed God by stopping a ay short. I only found relief after hiding myself in the secret place of His presence. When I asked God later why he wanted me to break the fast 1 day short, he only replied, "spiritual pride." He in His wisdom knew I would feel a great sense of accomplishment in making 40 days and possibly lose some of the spiritual benefit of drawing closer to Him in this fast.

Additional sources of shame: Feeling great disappointment when I've let someone else down or failed to gain their approval; when affection is withheld from me by someone significant to me; suffering from mental and emotional abuse; and enduring cruel, condescending nick-names. Perhaps a parent says, "Why are you so stupid; you'll never amount to anything. Why can't you be like so-and-so?" We are responsible for protecting our children from rejection and shame. We can't change our hurts from the past, but we can change and prevent the same hurts from happening to our families. I've met people so demented that they wanted to see their children go through some of the same hurts they had experienced – abuse, rape, divorce. They wanted someone else to hurt the way they had. That is twisted. We must protect and love our children. It is the work of the devil to put rejection on a child early, especially one destined for prophetic ministry or gifted in the spirit realm. If he can put the spirit of rejection on such a person, he'll tie up half his life trying to undo the damage even of things such as cutting words. That's why I watch what I say. We have to be careful how we treat each other. We need to show honor in our dealings with each other and our families.

Shame comes to victims of divorce and suicide by blaming themselves for things out of their control. The way we overcome it is by releasing our past and embracing the future in God. As long as you want to hold onto the past and just cling to all those mistakes and things you shouldn't have said, and what you could have done better, and all such poisonous ideas as "I could'a . . . I would'a . . . I should'a . . .," then they will keep your future stagnant. To embrace God's best, you've got to let yourself off the hook for your past.

The reason this is so powerful to me is that early in my Christian walk I did a lot of fasting to punish myself for falling short of the standard I felt God had set for me. I fasted and prayed to be rid of who I perceived myself to be. I hated myself. I couldn't forgive myself for things I had no control over. I couldn't forgive myself for what my father, an ordained minister, did to destroy me, my sister, our family, and our church. When I got around people who would ask questions, I would just bear the shame for his wrongs!

Thank God through the revelation of His Spirit and after much healing, now I simply fast and prayer

67

to draw closer to Him, know His ways and to simply know Him.

Shame has an unusual way of manifesting itself. In some people it is insecurity and inferiority complexes, in others it is superiority by trying to show "I'm something, I'm better than you." It is an aggressive, overpowering, and domineering spirit. Whatever its form, we all need healing.

When you stop blaming, punishing, and reminding yourself about the past and realize that God has forgiven you, then you can release and love others as you forgive yourself. In Matthew 18, the man couldn't forgive because his own voice was more real to him than the king's. The king says, "You're forgiven," while the man says, "I'll pay all." That's what is wrong with so many of us; we're still trying to pay for our mistakes. We do things out of service trying to earn acceptance. Find your worth in Him, not performance!

There are three motivational factors in life: fear, competition, and love. Fear will drive people, but it's not God's plan. Competition is powerful, and people go through all kinds of things for a trophy. But love is the greatest factor – it overcomes all. Paul said, "Forget those things that are behind." It is time to stop doing what you do to make up for something you didn't do! It is time to serve Him because you love Him. Reach for the promises. Rest in the loving arms of your Father and bask in His favor and acceptance, that's all you need.

3
Not Worthy But Trustworthy

God is accomplishing an apostolic revival, and part of that is not just Holy Ghost and healing – He is restoring our wounded mindsets and guilt-laden self identities. This phase is the releasing of ministries and gifts and the fulfilling of God's promise and commission on our lives. We need to get this lesson on self-forgiveness learned and move on to greater revival.

I used to have a German Shepherd dog that became sick. I took him to a veterinarian who sent us home with medication and treatment for him. Afterward he still seemed listless and sluggish, so I took him back to the vet. After running more tests, the veterinarian looked at him and said, "He should be fine – he shows no sign of sickness." He watched him in the cage for a moment and then said, "Aha!" He opened the cage, coaxed the dog out, and then gave him a big old kick in the rear. Suddenly the dog started leaping and jumping around the room. The moral of that story is that sometimes we just need a little motivation.

Unfortunately, some of the issues we've mentioned in this book occasionally cause some to sit in the "pig pen" of self-pity where they sit and mull over their sick past. This isn't our focus in addressing these issues – the point is that we can find the healing and liberation of His forgiveness. Stop looking for sympathy. Stop searching for excuses. Stop looking for someone else to cheer you up. Let me be the first to boot you out of your cage of despondency and into the sunshine of the bright future God has for you.

I have sat in some of the finest churches in Pentecost and thought, "They really have it together." However, it would amaze you to learn what one might find sitting in the pews. Sure, they dress finely and order themselves well, but it is beyond knowledge the past scars and hurts that have been endured. Even in churches that are twenty, thirty, or forty years old in maturity, you would think everything would be fine. But the pains, disappointments, hurts, and sorrows that exist in believers that have been serving God for many years, overwhelm me. A common deception from the enemy that we repeat is, "Time heals all wounds." Time simply passing does not heal wounds; if this were true, then I would not be spending hours helping 50 year old believers work thru issues that happened to them in their childhood. We have to make a focused, rational choice to forgive wounds and release the person('s) who have wounded us.

I believe it is God's intent and desire to bring complete inner healing. God wants His vessels to be in working order. You cannot be as effective in God's kingdom as He wants you to be if you have unresolved hurt, shame, bitterness, and resentment in your heart. God will leave you alone for a while, but He'll finally get down to the root of the matter. He'll put His hand directly on the very thing keeping you from growing and accomplishing what He would have you do. Why? Because He desires to heal us and for us to be effective powerful vessels in His kingdom. That is why He left His throne in glory and robed Himself in flesh and shed His blood for you and me – to bring healing to the bruised faith, shattered emotions, and broken dreams in our lives. God can put it back together again!

To review, when we have unforgiveness towards God, it produces rebellion in our lives. When we harbor unforgiveness towards our brother or sister, it produces bitterness. When we refuse to forgive our selves, we contend with guilt and shame. We talked about having unforgiveness towards others and the absolute necessity of forgiving and releasing others because of the prison it puts us in. We talked about forgiving and releasing God in areas of life that perhaps we don't understand quite why things happen the way they do, or why God blesses some others and seemingly our lives are not blessed. And then we talked about forgiving and releasing ourselves. Unresolved shame is one the most debilitating spiritual conditions with which we contend today. We talked about God allowing us to *agape* love – the kind of love we cannot humanly accomplish. This is the kind of love that only God can do through us. We cannot truly love God but must allow Him to love Himself through us. We cannot truly love our neighbors unless we allow God to love them through us with His agape love. And we can only truly love ourselves through God's agape love. It is His love.

Shame Destroys, Love Energizes

Shame destroys faith. Love energizes the greatest dimensions of faith. Galatians 5:6 says, "For in Jesus Christ neither circumcision availeth any thing, nor uncircumcision; but faith which worketh by love." I believe that we as the people of God have not seen the greatest dimension of Shekinah and revival that we desire to see because the dimension of God's love that

He desires for us has not yet been released in our midst. I believe when that dimension of love for God, love for souls, and love for His people is released, then we will see the dimension of faith released in our midst that will bring signs, wonders, and miracles.

The word "worketh" in the Greek is *energeo*, which means "to be operative, be at work, put forth power" (*Thayer's* 1754). I hear many people say, "Brother Arcovio, I believe God for it to happen" but do not step out I faith for the miracle. For so long we've operated in a measure of faith that's been below what God desires to release in our midst. When the faith is released that works by love – love with no agenda, love with no motive or reason, just simply love that God gives – then the miracle will happen because of the compassion that comes forth from the child of God.

It won't happen because you want to be spiritual, recognized by people, or for someone to say, "Oh, so-and-so prayed." It bothers me when someone says, "I got healed!" and another asks, "Really? Who was the preacher?" Or, "So many people got the Holy Ghost the other night." And someone responds, "Wow, who was preaching that night?" We put so much emphasis on those things sometimes that we take ourselves out of the dimension of true love – with no agenda or scheme.

True love gives willingly to those who absolutely will or can do nothing in return. It gives all for somebody who can do nothing to make you look better, to strengthen your position, or do anything in return for you. It gets down on its face weeping before God crying and interceding for lost souls. I believe one of elements that keeps the apostolic church from the greatest dimension of miracles is lack of honor. When we harbor unforgiveness we find it difficult to honor God or other others. We want to but our faith and obedience is hindered due to the pain and our not understanding what God is doing in our lives.

We see in Mark 6:1-6 that lack of honor directly affected the people's faith and ability to receive Jesus. This resulted in the hands of God manifested in the flesh hands being tied.

And he went out from thence, and came into his own country; and his disciples follow him. 2 And when the sabbath day was come, he began to teach in the synagogue: and many hearing him were astonished, saying, From whence hath this man these things? and what wisdom is this which is given unto him, that even such mighty works are wrought by his hands? 3 Is not this the carpenter, the son of Mary, the brother of James, and Joses, and of Juda, and Simon? and are not his sisters here with us? And they were offended at

76

him. 4 But Jesus said unto them, A prophet is not without honour, but in his own country, and among his own kin, and in his own house. 5 And he could there do no mighty work, save that he laid his hands upon a few sick folk, and healed them. 6 And he marvelled because of their unbelief. And he went round about the villages, teaching.

Verse six does not tell us that he *would* not do miracles. Rather it states He *could* there do not mighty work. Jesus considered their dishonor to be unbelief. When we do not forgive our selves then we do not feel we are worth of honor and end up dishonoring God who has chosen to anoint and use us. God knew what He was getting when He chose us! He has forgiven our past; we must honor what He did for us at Calvary by choosing to forgive our selves.

What is shame? Shame is the painful feeling of loss, the loss of respect for oneself, feelings of inadequacy or inferiority, the feeling that esteem and respect is lost in the eyes of those of significance in our lives, and the feelings of perceived or actual failure. The healed memories of the things we suffered in our past are not skeletons of shame, but they are testimonies of God's grace. Peter wrote, "Yet if *anyone suffers* as a Christian, let him not be ashamed, but let him glorify God in this matter" (1 Peter 4:16 *NKJV*). Shame wants you to hang your head when you think about everything that has happened that's out of your control – the divorce that took place although you did everything in your power to avoid it, the harm that came to you, or the abuse that had nothing to do with you. Shame makes you feel that somehow you are a lesser person in God's kingdom. Shame wants to tell you that you are defective. It wants you to think that people will reject you when they discover who you really are. That's what shame will do.

My desire is that you will be released from that lie, that the chains and yokes of shame will be broken from you, and that you'll realize those things you suffered can glorify God and be trophies of grace and glory. When we have come through the trial, through the wounding of our spirit and are healed, this produces sensitivity to those God brings us across that are wounded and we become instruments of His healing ministry. It's not through reaching down and pulling ourselves up by our own bootstraps. You'll never do enough good to overcome that heaviness you feel, my friend. You'll never fast enough, pray enough, or do enough. I come across people who drive themselves very hard, but neither their love for God nor a burden for souls motivates them – shame and guilt is what drives them on! They're trying to punish themselves or "work" for the kingdom of God to somehow gain His love and approval. We need to simply rest in His acceptance and love because we are His beloved son or daughter. I am loved and accepted simply because I am Hid child. When we understand this principle then we will fast and pray not to be accepted or receive something form God but, simply to know Him. Today God wants to release that shame by the overcoming power of His blood.

Healing Through the Blood of Jesus

It's not our work that gets it done, my friend. There can be healing only through His blood. We need a divine revelation of self-healing. I'm not talking about self-help here. The type of healing I'm talking about can only come through the blood of Jesus. You can't positive-think yourself out of this one. You can't do enough work for God. It is the blood of Jesus that has the power to deliver you. We need a divine revelation of healing in our lives. The Bible tells us in Hebrews 10:19, "Therefore, brethren, having boldness [confidence] to enter the Holiest by the blood of Jesus," (*NKJV*).

I don't enter because I've been going to church for twenty years. I don't have boldness because I've finally attained and arrived and have done everything just right. Instead, it's because, while I was a sinner, while I was a liar, while I was a thief, while I was a cheater, Christ died for me! And when He shed His blood, I became holy because He is holy. Through obedience to His Word I repented of my sins, was baptized in His name, and received the overcoming power of His Spirit. I then can say with Paul; I can do all things through Christ which strengtheneth me. (Philippians 4:13)

Shame will tell you "you're worthless." Shame will say "you're nobody." The devil loves to introduce false humility. During my youth, I grew up hearing preachers who thought it was really, really something big to get up and say, "I'm a worm, I'm unworthy, I'm nobody." Listen, my friend, He made you worthy by His blood. Undeserving? Yes! Unworthy? Never! The blood of Jesus makes us worthy. You want to know how much you are worthy, my friend? You want to know how valuable you are? Jesus signed your worth with the signature of His blood at Calvary. He gave it all because you've valuable to Him. You're worthy!

We need to get rid of this man-made idea of "I'm unworthy." It's a shame. What we're really trying to say is, "I don't want to do God's work. I don't have enough faith that God can do it through me because I'm unworthy, because my dad abused me, because

80

my mom was an alcoholic, because I came from an abused home, because I'm not a preacher's kid, because I used to be a drug addict, because I used to be a biker, because I was a prostitute," or whatever our excuse.

And when you sit on a pew and the preacher talks about great revival, you'll relegate it to somebody else; you'll say "it's for someone else." No, my friend, you are mighty in God! You are a child of God. You are a chosen vessel. You are made worthy by His blood.

Shame doesn't just separate us from family and friends. It cuts us out of the presence of God as well. The blood of Christ, however, reconciles us. "But now in Christ Jesus," it says, "you who once were far off have been brought near by the blood of Christ" (Ephesians 2:13 *NKJV*). When we are truly healed by the blood, we can become an instrument of healing to others. Shame-based mentality will tell you "you're unworthy." But you've got to answer that lie by saying, "His blood has made me worthy." Say this out loud right now, "His blood has made me worthy." When we live with shame-based mentalities, we begin to idolize preachers and put them on pedestals because we think somehow they've attained worthiness. "I don't know how they got it, but they are worthy." Listen, my friend, God's not looking for worthiness. He's looking

81

for trustworthiness. He's looking for someone He can trust with His greatness. He's just looking for someone He can trust with His anointing, with His greatest gifts. He's not looking for pedigrees. He's not looking for who's done it right. He's looking for somebody who can just trust in His power. This is the fallacy that trips us up when we feel that somehow a 21 day fast or prayer vigil qualifies us. We are qualified by His choosing and blood. All fasting and prayer but be to draw closer to Him and know His ways.

Several years ago I had the opportunity in Ethiopia to sit down with Brother Billy Cole personally for several hours. I said, "Brother Cole, in a small package if you can, give me the reason why God has allowed you to be so successful in praying people through to the Holy Ghost and seeing revival across the world in crusades." He said, "Get a pen out." So I did. "First of all, know where God's working. Secondly, know when God's working. Third, show up with the right attitude of faith." That's our problem sometimes; we know God has called us, we know what He's doing, but we show up and don't know if it's going to happen. We sit back with our arms folded and we say, "Okay, God, prove it to me. Okay, pull it out of the hat. Let me see a miracle. Oh, come on, let me see something happen." Or we say, "who am I for God to use me in such a great manner?"

Right Attitudes Necessary

Let me tell you something; we need to come to the house of God with the right attitude of faith, come with expectancy. Come saying, "God, I believe you will deliver my family. I believe you are healing my life. I believe you are going to fill someone with the Holy Ghost."

Then Brother Cole said, "When it happens, don't get drunk." Don't get so drunk on your success that you think you're something in God. Recognize your source is always the power of His Spirit. Stay humble before God and it will happen. With the right attitude, you are not far from something awesome in God and being mightily used in the Holy Ghost. I want to impart something to you to build your faith: God anoints flesh and blood. Think about it: Holiness anoints clay! Shekinah can rest on simple vessels.

Don't ever, ever underestimate the power of the blood of Jesus. Exodus 12:12-13 says, 12."For I will pass through the land of Egypt on that night, and will strike all the firstborn in the land of Egypt, both man and beast; and against all the gods of Egypt I will execute judgment: I *am* the LORD. 13."Now the blood shall be a sign for you on the houses where you *are*. And when I see the blood, I will pass over you; and the plague shall not be on you to destroy *you . . .*' " (*NKJV*).

When someone says, "Yes, God can do it for so-and-so but not for me." What they're really saying is, "God doesn't have enough power in His blood to deliver me." Some believe God can deliver the alcoholic, "But I just don't know," they worry, "that I can be delivered." Don't ever underestimate the power of the blood. When you plead that blood, you release anointing. Mother, when you plead that blood over your child, it takes just the mere words by faith, "I plead the blood over my son." When you lay your hand on the pillow of that husband while he's at work and plead the blood, there's power in that! Hell trembles when you plead the blood.

God had commissioned the death angel who went through all the nation of Egypt with a sword of vengeance and slew thousands of the first born. Oh, the sorrow and crying that went up that night! Can I remind you that this angel was a death angel commissioned by God. However, you see, when they put the blood of a lamb over the doorpost and lintel, that death angel could not cross over that blood. He had to pass on by. Not even a death angel commissioned by God can cross the bloodline. There is not a devil in hell or a demonic force on Earth that can cross the threshold of the blood of Jesus applied to your life! Don't live in fear if you plead the blood over your life and your family. The devil cannot cross it – he lacks the power.

Fighting Demons

When I feel I'm in warfare with the devil, I don't get nervous. Some people talk about fighting the devil, wrestling with him, knocking lamps over, and busting mirrors. They get up in the morning with their tie sideways and their hair all messed up, and they have bumps and bruises and rips in their clothes – "Bless God, I was fighting the devil last night." That's not necessary. You see, when the devil comes around, I don't get nervous because greater is He that is in me. I am not resting in self-confidence but rather God-confidence. I walk in confidence of what God can and will do thru me. That has never changed. The gates of hell will never prevail against this church. I don't care how great the devil tries to be, what's inside of you is greater. That blood that Jesus shed is greater. That power of the Holy Ghost on your soul is greater than the devil tormenting your family, stealing your job, and aggravating your ulcers. Quit sitting there and letting the devil push you around. You've got the blood, you've got the Name! You've got the power of the Holy Ghost. If you allow the enemy to choose the battleground, he will always choose the mind. It is there that he can be victorious. We have the mind of Christ. When we walk in daily intimacy with Christ, we walk in confidence and victory. Our identity is in Him, not our self or past.

I've done this in foreign countries. When I first arrive in a country and arrive at the hotel and I sense warfare, I get up and anoint with oil. If I don't have any oil, I anoint with my tears. I anoint the four walls of the hotel room where I will sleep. I say, "I plead the blood of Jesus over this room," and I can sleep peacefully. I remember the first time I went to the Philippines; I went to an area bound by witchcraft. Demonic forces were powerful in that city. The devil didn't know what was fixing to hit that area – they'd never had a Holy Ghost outpouring in that city. They'd never had a crusade there.

When I got there I was deathly sick. We had to drive 13 hours over a bumpy dirt road. By the time I got there, my body ached from the top of my head to the bottom of my feet, partially because of the tropical flu I was fighting and partially because I was just utterly exhausted. I said, "Lord, I need a good night's sleep for this crusade." I was so ill I only had the strength to check into my hotel and collapse into bed. The weather was about 102 degrees and felt like 300% humidity. It is miserable being sick with the flu in that setting!

In my room a little air conditioner was doing its best to do something, although I don't know what it was doing. It felt like it was making the room hotter. I got up a few times to check to see if the heat was on because hot air was coming out of that thing. It was making such an awful racket. If I turned it off, though, the room felt like it was closing in on me. At least the poor thing kept a little circulation going in the room.

Finally, I started to drift off to a fitful sleep. Suddenly I heard somebody bang, bang, bang, on my door. I jumped out of bed and threw my robe on and thought, *what's going on? Maybe one of the team members has had an emergency.* There was a sixty-five year old elder on the trip with us whose health came to mind – I thought maybe he'd had a heart attack or something; I just didn't know. So I opened the door and looked out, and nobody was there. I thought, *somebody is playing with me.* So I shut the door, latched it, and lay back down.

I had just dozed off, and it happened again about twenty minutes later. I jumped up as before, but nobody was there. I started to get very annoyed, but I lay back down. After about thirty minutes, all of a sudden – God is my witness – I heard the crunch of footsteps approaching my door. So I slipped out of bed, put my housecoat on, and eased the chain back and unlocked the door. Then "in Jesus' Name" I grabbed the broomstick by my bed. Between me and Jesus and the broomstick, we were going to get the thing figured out!

I opened the door, and . . . nobody was standing there! Chills went up my back as I realized what I was up against. I said, "Ah, okay devil," and shut the door. At the same time, the electricity went off – "bang!" And the air conditioner just went "bang!"

Pleading the Blood of Jesus

Now I'm not a "macho man", and, as I stood there, my heart started fluttering rapidly. I was supposed to be a great man of God here to have a crusade, and I was scared to death. So, I gathered my wits and took the bottle of oil I carry and began to anoint the walls. I would say, "I plead your blood, Jesus. I plead your blood over this entire room."

I anointed every wall, every mirror, doorknob, and even the air conditioner. God is my witness that, when I anointed the air conditioner, the electricity kicked back on, and that little machine started blow-ing ice cold air! All the team members who came that week said, "Man, your room's cold!" I had the best room of the team because I cast the devil out of the air conditioner!

I believe in pleading the blood. I can't tell you how many times I've prayed over the church I pastored walking the aisles and anointing pews, chairs, and walls just pleading the blood. Why? When you plead the blood, demonic forces are broken. Spirits that would try to come and torment are driven off and victory comes. Plead the blood over your life! Plead the blood over your vehicles! Plead the blood over your home! Plead the blood over your spouse! Plead the blood over your children! Plead the blood over your job! Just plead the blood!

In 2003 while I was the pastor of the church in St. Joseph, Missouri, the church was going thru a terrible time of disunity and confusion. One night I awoke at 2 am with my heart just pounding in my chest and sweat pouring down. I sat straight up in bed and the only way I can describe what I felt was, it was as if a huge beast was standing over the church getting ready to devour it. I think I understand what Paul meant when he wrote in 1 Corinthians 15:32; 2 If after the manner of men I have fought with beasts at Ephesus...

I softly told my wife that I was going to the church to pray. As I walked the aisles of the church, travailing and praying in the spirit, I felt this spiritual heaviness begin to lift. I anointed every pew, the walls...everything. Then I walked out into the darkness of the church parking lot and with Holy Ghost boldness I began to adjure the principalities of St. Joseph pleading the blood of Jesus against them. Suddenly up on the hillside where a fence joined the property with an open field, I heard a bloodcurdling scream that sent chills to my very bones. When I looked up, I saw two red eyes glaring at me. Now my feet wanted to turn and run back into the church but the Holy Spirit rose up in me and I stared right into those eyes and said, "Devil, is that all you got?" I locked my eyes with whatever was on the top of that hill screaming at me and began walking towards it calling on the theme of Jesus. The "thing" gave one more piercing scream and then was gone. I immediately felt the most incredible peace settle over the area. That Sunday's services were the freest we had ever had and God brought great unity in the church. We witnessed over 100 filled with the Holy Ghost in a short period. Yes, spiritual warfare is a reality and so is the authority we have in Christ through His blood!

God wants you to be whole again through the washing of His blood. I wish I could just pull people over the edge into the beauty and glory of His perfect will. When Jesus opened up the Bible at the beginning of His ministry, He released to us, the anointed, our mandate. He said, "The Spirit of the Lord *is* upon me, because he hath anointed me to preach the gospel to the poor; he hath sent me to heal the brokenhearted, to preach deliverance to the captives, and recovering of sight to the *[spiritually]* blind, to set at liberty them that are bruised," (Luke 4:18). The bruised are those with life-shattering experiences that have taken them captive. God has anointed us for that reason. When people come through the church doors with lives shattered by sin feeling bruised, broken, and captive, God's people need to be to the point where they are healed and ready to minister to the hurting. We must release anointing so that others may be healed.

Many people suffer depression because of shame. Depression is not a human emotion – it's a frame of mind influenced by demonic attacks. The Bible refers to depression as the *spirit of heaviness*. Isaiah 61 gives the remedy for depression: the oil of joy for mourning, beauty for ashes (abuse), and the garment of praise for the spirit of heaviness.

When God destroys the yoke of shame off His children, then He can fulfill His promise. Joel's promise in 2:26-28 is, 26."You shall eat in plenty and be satisfied, And praise the name of the LORD your God, Who has dealt wondrously with you; And My people shall **never be put to shame**. 27.Then you shall know that I *am* in the midst of Israel: I *am* the LORD your God And there is no other." And He says again, "My people shall **never be put to shame**." Then He says further, 28."And it shall come to pass afterward . . ." – after what? After the healing and restoration and after the shame has been lifted. Then, ". . . I will pour out My Spirit on **all flesh**; Your sons and your daughters shall prophesy, Your old men shall dream dreams, Your young men shall see visions" (*NKJV*). (Emphasis added.)

When God has released our lives, when He has healed us, when shame has been abolished, when His love begins to flow through us in a measure like never before, then His blessings and anointings will begin to flow.

God is ready to move the church into the "afterward" dimension of apostolic demonstration.

4
Innocence and Shame

In the sixth chapter of Judges we learn that the children of Israel's lifestyle had been severely cramped by an invading army. The Midianites were taking all their crops, and Israel was feeding on scraps and crumbs. Even what little bit they could salvage, they had to hide so the Midianites couldn't get it. However, God's people should have been feasting instead!

I'm so sick and tired of seeing God's children live in defeat. I'm tired of seeing God's children, who have the right of the kingdom, die at empty banquet tables, when there are tables available that have been set with God's anointing and blessing. Why do people settle for the scraps of only what the devil will allow them to have? As I travel across America, I see so many Pastor's, Leader's and Minister's who struggle with fear and intimidation. They are stripped of their God ordained anointing and authority while they cower in front of controlling board members or intimidating church members. The enemy wants to convince you that he has the power and authority over you when the truth is we have the power and authority over all the power of the enemy. This was afforded to us by the blood of Calvary. God's promise in the book of Revelations to those who overcome Jezebel and it's intimidations is, "power over the nations." Revelations 2:26 records; "And he that overcometh, and keepeth my works unto the end, to him will I give power over the nations."

Jesus said in Luke 10:19; "Behold, I give unto you power to tread on serpents and scorpions, and over all the power of the enemy: and nothing shall by any means hurt you."

In Genesis the situation of the "yet to be created earth", was described as "darkness covering the face of the deep." This darkness was not the darkness that occurs when light is not present but rather spiritual darkness. The word darkness was translated from the from the Hebrew word *choshek* (kho-shek'); which has the meaning; the dark; hence (literally) darkness; figuratively, misery, destruction, death, ignorance, sorrow, wickedness:[i]

In verse two, God said, "Let there be light." This was not the light of the sun, moon or stars, as they were not created until verse 14. This light was the light of the Glory of God that dispels spiritual darkness.

However, the fallen archangel, Lucifer, the prince and power of the air (atmosphere), which had fallen from the heavens and upon earth in the form of a serpent. It was in this setting of spiritual darkness that God created mankind. Genesis 1:26 records; "And God said; Let us make man in our image, after our likeness: and let them have *dominion* (emphasis mine) over the fish of the sea, and over the fowl of the air, and over the cattle, and over all the earth, and over every creeping thing that keepeth upon the earth."

God created Adam placed him in the midst of spiritual darkness and gave him dominion over all the power of the enemy. Even thought the first Adam lost that dominion due to his and Eve's disobedience to the commandment of God, the second Adam (Jesus Christ) purchased that dominion back thru the blood He shed at Calvary! 1 Corinthians 15:22 records; "For as in Adam all die, even so in Christ shall all be made alive."

We talk about a church triumphant, a church victorious, but I watch God's children cower down in fear. They're afraid the enemy going to take their husband, their family, their job, or this or that. As long as we are in Christ and doing His will, the enemy cannot

95

touch us, unless the Lord permits it for our molding. The reason the children of Israel were so defeated was that they had disobeyed God's Word. They were out of order with God's will. 1 John 2:17 says;"And the world passes away and disappears, and with it the forbidden cravings (the passionate desires, the lust) of it; but he who does the will of God and carries out His purposes in his life abides (remains) forever." (AMP)

The devil cannot touch you if you are in God's will and are walking in His Word. 1 John 5:18 records; "We know [absolutely] that anyone born of God does not [deliberately and knowingly] practice committing sin, but the One Who was begotten of God carefully watches over and protects him [Christ's divine presence within him preserves him against the evil], and the wicked one does not lay hold (get a grip) on him or touch [him]." (AMP)

That's why David said, "Fix my steps, Lord! Order my steps according to your Word." That's why the children of Israel were impoverished because they had not obeyed the voice of the Lord nor were they walking in the revealed will of God.

God wants to come into the midst of that fear, into the midst of that bondage, into the midst of that torment and reveal Himself as Jehovah-Shalom – the God of Peace. Many men and women of God don't even know His peace. They live with torment in their spirits, and the enemy knows that fear and faith cannot mix. God hasn't given us the *spirit of fear* but of power and of love and of a sound mind. Fear and intimidation are spirits. If you're bound by fear, then you don't have any power, you don't know how to love, and your mind is tormented!

However, through the power of God, you are going to receive deliverance – He will release the peace of His Spirit into your spirit, into your life, and into your home. The answer to the *spirit of fear* is to walk in the confidence of power of the Spirit that can only come from walking in the daily revealed word and will of God. When we walk in the spirit we do not walk in confidence of our flesh nor directed by our emotions and will. Galatians 5:25 says; "If we live by the [Holy] Spirit, let us also walk by the Spirit. [If by the Holy Spirit we have our life in God, let us go forward walking in line, our conduct controlled by the Spirit.]" (AMP)

Galatians 2:20 records; "I have been crucified with Christ [in Him I have shared His crucifixion]; it is no longer I who live, but Christ (the Messiah) lives in me; and the life I now live in the body I live by faith in (by adherence to and reliance on and complete trust in) the Son of God, Who loved me and gave Himself up for me." (AMP)

True confidence and power through Christ can only be found through *brokenness. Brokenness* can be defines as, "total dependence on the power of God."

The second answer to the *spirit of fear* is to walk in the *agape love* of the Holy Spirit. This love cannot be humanly obtained or produced; it is the love of God that is shed abroad in our hearts by the Holy Spirit (Romans 5:5). When we rest in His complete love and acceptance this defeats the *spirit of fear* that often manifests itself thru the intimidation and control of man. Proverbs 29:25 records; "The fear of man bringeth a snare: but whoso putteth his trust in the Lord shall be safe."

The Bible tells us in the book of John that Jesus said "the Comforter . . . *is* the Holy Ghost" (John 14:26). That comforter means one who assists or comes alongside to make up where we lack – to fill in the gaps where we have weakness or inability. Then He said, "Peace I leave with you, my peace I give unto you: not as the world giveth, give I unto you. *Let not* your heart be troubled, neither let it be afraid" (14:27). God will give us His peace but, we choose to walk in it. It is our duty to not *let* our hearts become troubled.

The third answer to the *spirit of fear* is a sound mind. The word sound is derived from the Greek word;

sophronismos (so-fron-is-mos'); from NT:4994; which has the meaning-discipline, i.e. selfcontrol:[ii]

We must exercise self-discipline to refuse to let our hearts become trouble by the fears and intimidations that the spirit of fear brings. We walk in soundness of mind with our confidence in Christ.

A while back God began to open this to me because I lived a very troubled and fearful existence as a result of abuse I suffered when I was a child. God began to magnify this and transform so many areas of my life through His power, love and having a sound mind. When I minister, I often notice spirits of fear, bondage, and depression binding God's people, who actually are trying to serve Him. My heart longs and yearns to see others experience the deliverance and the transformation that God has produced in my life.

Peace the World Can't Give

The peace He's talking about is not the kind of peace that the world gives. The peace the world is looking for is an existence with no turmoil, war, or heartache. That existence can only be found in eternity with Jesus. Earth will never experience such peace, for even now it groans and faces destruction with fervent heat (Romans 8:23 and 2 Peter 3:10). Everything we know, everything constituting our existence, will one day be completely consumed and obliterated in the fiery heat of God's wrath and judgment. The only ones who will know peace are those prepared to meet Him when He comes by having washed their robes with the blood He shed on Calvary, by submitting their lives to the power of His Spirit, and by walking daily in His word – those are the ones who will know the peace of eternal life with Him.

The kind of peace that God wants us to know today is the peace in the middle of the storm, that calm assurance while the trouble is still brewing, the stillness that remains in spite of all the problems around us – it's the peace of knowing "I am His and He is mine."

It's found in the joy of knowing that the righteousness of God has become your righteousness. We fail when we try to serve God with our righteousness. The Scripture says all our righteousness is as filthy rags (Isaiah 64:6). You know why? There is nothing we can do that can work for righteousness. There is a difference between righteousness and holiness. Righteousness is a gift from God. The actual word "righteous" means to be innocent[iii]. You see, the basic problem with so many people of God is that they go to

God's house and sing the songs, but deep down a voice tells them, "You're still filthy! You're still dirty. You're still guilty. You're still the failure you've always been. You're still nobody. You'll never be amount to anything!" We come to the house of God, paint our smile on, and talk about faith while we're still tormented by the thoughts and failures of yesterday. Or worse yet, we fast and pray thinking these works will somehow make us righteous. We're still tormented by the lifestyles we were forced to live because of choices we made that can never, ever be changed. Because of that, we live bound and our faith is bound. That's why we don't see miracles like we need to see.

Somehow we believe that we still are not righteous, that God still doesn't accept us. He doesn't love us enough to heal us; He doesn't love us enough to do it for us. But now that spirit will be broken. God is delivering you, healing you, and giving you His peace, His righteousness, and the innocence of His Spirit. Fasting and prayer are not to obtain *what we need*, but rather it is to know Him in a deeper relationship of intimacy.

He said, "My peace I give you." I can't tell you how long I struggled trying to be righteous in myself. Daily I tried to convince the devil and myself that I wasn't guilty. There were times just driving down the highway I'd feel the taunts and jeers of the enemy for circumstances in which I knew my hands were innocent, and I knew my heart was right. I fasted and prayer feeling that somehow if I "paid" a heavy enough price, I would find peace. Don't ever let the enemy choose the battleground, for he will always choose the battleground of the mind. It is in the mind where Satan wins many victories. If you let him, the devil will browbeat you for things you have no control over. We have the *mind of Christ* (1 Corinthians 2:16)! Walk in it!

Sometimes I would just cry out and say, "Forgive me, Jesus," for no other reason than because I felt guilty, I felt weighed down, I felt like I was not innocent. My prayers were weighed down. I could believe God for everyone else, but I couldn't believe God would do things for me.

The devil works overtime to convince you that you're still guilty. He doesn't mind for you to believe that you're forgiven (the western concept of being forgiven, is being "pardoned.)" For example, when a governor pardons someone for a crime, they are released from the penalty, but the crime, however, remains on their record permanently – still guilty. The enemy doesn't mind people believing they are forgiven as long as, in their minds, the sin is still there. The truth is we were not only forgiven (pardoned) but made innocent by the blood of Christ! Colossians 2:13-14 says; 13"And you, being dead in your sins and the uncircumcision of your flesh, hath he quickened together with him, having forgiven you all trespasses;14 Blotting out the handwriting of ordinances that was against us, which was contrary to us, and took it out of the way, nailing it to his cross;

The following is in reference to "Blotting out the hand-writing of ordinances." By the hand-writing of ordinances the apostle most evidently means the ceremonial law: this was against them, for they were bound to fulfil it; and it was contrary to them, as condemning them for their neglect and transgression of it. This law God himself has blotted out. Blotting out the hand-writing is probably an allusion to Num 5:23, where the curses written in the book, in the case of the woman suspected of adultery, are directed to be blotted out with the bitter waters. And there can be little doubt of a further allusion, namely, to the custom of discharging the writing from parchment by the application of such a fluid as the muriatic acid, which immediately dissolves those ferruginous calces which constitute the blackening principle of most inks. But the East India inks, being formed only of simple black, such as burnt ivory, or cork, and gum water, may be wiped clean off from the surface of the paper or parchment by the application of a wet sponge, so as to leave not one legible vestige remaining: this I have often proved.[iv]

I know of people who have lost their innocence – people who suffered from some mistake or failure – and they waste the rest of their lives thinking they will never amount to anything because they are no longer innocent. You see, that is why Christ went to Calvary, to erase the condemnation of our past and restore our innocence through His blood. When we walk daily in intimacy with Him, we escape the condemnations of the enemy. Romans 8:1 records; "HEREFORE, [there is] now no condemnation (no adjudging guilty of wrong) for those who are in Christ Jesus, who live [and] walk not after the dictates of the flesh, but after the dictates of the Spirit." (AMP)

Christ Became Our Sin

The Bible says that He became sin so that we who do sin might become righteous (2 Corinthians 5:21). Righteousness means innocence – that we might know "I am innocent." Even though I may have failed, I know that I am innocent because of the gift of God. You cannot work for righteousness, my friend. Holiness is what you strive toward: "Be ye holy for I am holy." That is why we put in the daily effort to employ God's Word and let it transform us. Righteousness, the innocence that God gives us, comes the moment His Name washes our sins away. 1 Corinthians 6:11 records; "And such some of you were [once]. But you were washed clean (purified by a complete atonement for sin and made free from the guilt of sin), and you were consecrated (set apart, hallowed), and you were justified [pronounced righteous, by trusting] in the name of the Lord Jesus Christ and in the [Holy] Spirit of our God." (AMP)

In God's eyes you become innocent-just as though you had never sinned.

Yet we struggle to accept that innocence because we try to work for it, fast for it, and pray for it. Why? Because we still feel guilty, dirty, and unworthy. We feel we have to go to great lengths to convince God, convince the world, and convince ourselves that we're innocent. We're as filthy rags – we'll always feel filthy and dirty until we receive His innocence and walk in the confidence gained by daily intimacy with Him. The Bible tells us in Romans 4:5, "But to him that worketh not, but believeth on him that justifieth the ungodly, his faith is counted for righteousness" (*KJV*). Abraham believed, and it was his faith that was counted as righteousness, not his works! "Even as David also describeth the blessedness of the man, unto whom God imputeth righteousness [*giving it freely*] without works" (4:6). You can't work for righteousness, my friend. You can't work to make yourself better or cleaner than what Christ has already done.

We are a lot like the ten lepers standing outside the temple crying, "Jesus, have mercy on us.". We say, "Oh God, forgive me!" And then, when we're forgiven and rejoice, are baptized and believe our sins are washed away, and are filled with His Spirit, we go forth into a new life. But somehow, as the days go by, something begins to creep back into our spirits making us still feel guilt for our past. The devil will still try to convince us we are guilty because of the twists and turns we've made in the past, that we'll never amount to what God wanted to do in and for us, and that we'll never quite make the fullness of what God wants.

God would not allow the priest to enter into the holiest place if they had a scab which represented leprosy. Leviticus 13:7-8

7 But if the scab spread much abroad in the skin, after that he hath been seen of the priest for his cleansing, he shall be seen of the priest again:

8 And if the priest see that, behold, the scab spreadeth in the skin, then the priest shall pronounce him unclean: it is a leprosy.

A man with leprosy could not enter the into the holy place. Do you know what a scab is? It's an un-healed wound.

You see, there are situations in our lives that we have to submit to God. We can't explain why they happen, but we've got to let God heal and take the pain, bitterness, and hurt away. Even though the devil still screams at us and says, "You're guilty! You're guilty!" Even though he points his finger in our face and says, "You'll never amount to anything!" we've got to receive God's righteousness – His innocence – by faith. We cannot enter into the best God has for us if we harbor a "scab" or an *unhealed wound.*

Nine of the ten lepers who came to Jesus left cleansed, but the tenth came back and worshipped Je-sus. Through the intimacy of worship he was not only cleansed but was made whole. We too are made whole by our intimacy with Christ! What was he made whole of? Not only was his physical body made whole of the scars that the leprosy had left on him, but he was also made whole of the pain and the shame of what it meant to be a leper – "unclean! unclean!" He'd grown so accustomed to hanging his head in shame, shouting those words to the world. Now he was freed from that association! I wonder how many nights the other nine woke up in a cold sweat after dreaming they were still lepers and found the word "unclean!" on their lips. Even though they were cleansed, for many years they shied away from the crowd afraid they would be rejected because they expected it. They still identified with their shame. We must not identify with the wounding and failures of our past, we must identify with Jesus Christ! Maybe there are things in your past that are so horrifying: situations you were bound by or mistakes you made. You can keep those things so fresh in your mind, and fear so greatly that someone will find out, that you shun the crowd. You convince yourself that God will never use you. You remember the shame of it all.

But, what that one leper found – the intimacy and relationship with Jesus – made him whole. He was loosed from the shame and the terror of being a leper. And you can be too. Cry out to God, thank Him for His forgiveness, beg for His wholeness, and be washed in the intimacy of His Spirit. Find your identity in Christ!

Accepted By His Righteousness

There are men and women of God who are faithful. Their hands are clean; their hearts are right, but, somehow, they've convinced themselves that they don't belong. Psalm 24:3-5 says, [3]."Who shall ascend into the hill of the LORD? or who shall stand in his holy place? [4].He that hath clean hands, and a pure heart; who hath not lifted up his soul unto vanity, nor sworn deceitfully. [5].He shall receive the blessing from the LORD, and righteousness from the God of his salvation."

You see, we don't understand how much God wants to bless our lives because, somehow, we feel we still have not yet received the acceptance and the cleansing from God. Our prayers are not prayers of faith – they're still prayers that attempt to climb some imaginary ladder trying to earn His acceptance. Let me tell you something that you should never forget: all you have to do is put your hands in His and say, "Lord, I receive your innocence." That's it. Simply rest in the peace found in the fact, "I am His son/daughter, He loves me." You can't impress Him enough, you can't win enough souls, you can't give enough money, you can't fast enough days, and you could never pray enough hours to earn it, because it's a gift-His gift of love. Romans 5:8-9 records; 8 But God shows and clearly proves His [own] love for us by the fact that while we were still sinners, Christ (the Messiah, the Anointed One) died for us. 9 Therefore, since we are

109

now justified (acquitted, made righteous, and brought into right relationship with God) by Christ's blood, how much more [certain is it that] we shall be saved by Him from the indignation and wrath of God. (AMP)

He gives us His innocence because of who He is, not because of anything we are or could ever become through our own efforts

It is time to unstop the fountain of God's blessings. We fail to receive them because, somehow, we believe we're not innocent – not righteous – enough.

Right now, In Jesus Name, I command you to be loosed in the Holy Ghost; I loose you from every condemning voice. I loose you from every spirit of guilt and shame. Say it now, "I receive the innocence of God. I receive your righteousness purchased by your blood. It doesn't matter if I was a prostitute, I'm holy. It doesn't matter if I was a young person who destroyed my life, I'm holy. I'm righteous because of You, Lord."

Luke 1:74 says, "That he would grant unto us, that we being delivered out of the hand of our enemies might serve him without fear!" You cannot be completely delivered from the enemy until you can serve Jesus Christ fearlessly. You don' have to wake up each morning with a sense of dread. We shouldn't think that when a rock cracks the windshield we would feel,

"Oh, what have I done wrong now?" Some people serve God with the constant worry about the next misstep – when is God going to judge me again, when will He bring something against my life? Your child becomes sick and you think "God's judging me." By the blood of Jesus I release you from that mindset so you may serve God without terror! We do need to fear (respect-2 Corinthians 7:1) the Lord, but we should not be bound with the terror that brings condemnation. You are loosed from the grip and the stranglehold of the enemy.

You see, that passage in Luke, along with the next verse, make a complete thought: 74."... that we being delivered out of the hand of our enemies might serve him without fear, 75.In holiness and righteousness before him, all the days of our life" (1:74-75). How do we serve Him in holiness (Divine consecration)? We serve Him in holiness by obeying His Word.

Hebrews 12:14 records; Strive to live in peace with everybody and pursue that consecration and holiness without which no one will [ever] see the Lord. (AMP)

The word *holiness* in this verse is deried from the Greek word *hagiasmos* (hag-ee-as-mos'); from NT:37; which has then meanings-properly, purification, i.e. (the state) purity; concretely (by Hebraism) a purifier:[v]

However, the only way we can serve Him in righteousness is not by our righteousness. I've seen people who dressed the part and did everything they could on the outside, but they lived under bondage – their faith was bound. Often a true believers faith has been bound for years by this principle of "self-righetousness." Some groups can go out there and see tremendous miracles because in their ignorance they receive the righteousness of God by faith. They believe that God will bless them. I'm sick and tired of seeing that happen all over the world and not happen in our own midst. It is time for that spirit of fear or doubt to be broken and God's people loosed! The sons and daughters of God are to worship and serve Him without fear but in the righteousness and innocence of God. Say right now, "I receive it!" You may not feel anything emotional right now, but just claim it by faith.

Open Wounds

Do you know why some husbands are not able to love their wives or receive them? Or why some wives are not able to receive love from their husbands? It's because of past wounds that haven't been healed. There are ministries that will never ascend into the supernatural because of past wounds they've covered over and the acid of bitterness, rebellion and shame that eats at their spirit. They've learned to just go through the motions – abuses, incest, molestations, and mental abuses that have so scarred and blocked their ability to love and to give love that they are spiritual zombies. They repeat the rhetoric of the word but never receive the healing truths into their spirit. They mentally "know the word" but do not walk in intimacy with the giver of the Word. The only answer is the righteousness of God. It's got to be faith in your heart.

I've tried to help people whose lives were so messed up but, I knew I could not help them unless I could get them to believe they were pure and innocent simply because of His blood. It's not because they fasted twenty-four hours or twenty-four days or because they prayed all night. It's because of the righteousness of God. When they climb the made up ladders I their mind because of their own works, then when they make a mistake, they "fall" all the way to the bottom of bondage by condemnation.

We talk so much about power, yet we've skipped over something so vital- walking in the Spirit. We're gaining anointing and authority, but we don't know what to do with it all because we're still living in shame and guilt. The devil doesn't have to bind you with alcohol and drugs if he can simply just keep you bound by your past. It's just like the man who owed a large sum of money to his lord (Mathew 18:23-35). The lord commanded that he and his wife and family and all that he had be sold to satisfy the debt. We owed a debt of sin we could never pay and our Lord could have done with us, but He didn't.

After the servant begged for a chance to pay the debt, the lord said, "Loose him and forgive him of his debt," yet all he heard was that he was going to be loosed; he never heard the word "forgive" because he didn't believe that he was forgiven. He never believed that he was innocent. He left the king's presence still carrying that turmoil. That's what made him grab the man that owed him so little and demand repayment. You cannot love others until you get over the thought that you're a failure and a "nobody." That's what we do when we choose to hold a grudge against someone who has wronged us, even after we have been forgiven so much. We cannot have the spirit to forgive until we truly understand how much we have been forgiven. Any form of un-forgiveness delivers us back over to the "tormentors" (spirits of regret and condemnation). Paul understood this truth as evident in his writings in Colossians 3:13; "Forbearing one another, and forgiving one another, if any man have a quarrel against any:

even as Christ forgave you, so also do ye." (emphasis mine).

You're still telling yourself that you'll never make it. And, although God has put the sky as the limit, you have put a limit to what God can do in your life because your faith will only take you that far.

Deliverance Through Honesty

Deliverance comes because of honesty. Will you be honest and say, "The Holy Spirit has been talking to my heart through this?

Many people look at the doors God is opening to our ministry in this hour and say, "Oh, he has it made." He is connected to the right people and gets all the right breaks. As a matter of fact, when most people observe a dream being fulfilled and do not know the history of the person, they do not perceive the long dusty roads walked, the pain and sacrifice endured to see a dream fulfilled. This is why I love to get to "know" a man or woman of God who is being mightily used. I want to know what Paul Harvey calls, "The rest of the story." You can usually spot a vessel that has "been through the fire", because God's anointed "walk with a limp (i.e. Jacob after his face o face encounter with the angel of the Lord at Peniel in Genesis 32:24-32) There are people who don't know the horror of my background. They don't know the horror of the things that I've done or the things that have been done to me. I'm a walking trophy of the grace and mercy of God. I can only walk in the confidence of the innocence and peace of God.

You see, the same God who revealed Himself as Jehovah-Shalom- The Lord our Peace, is the same God that revealed Himself as Jehovah-Tsidkenu – the Lord our Righteousness. This is something we have skipped over and danced around for years in our movement. We shout and dance about healing of the physical. We shout and dance when someone's tumor disappears or when someone gets out of a wheelchair. We kick pews over and swing from the chandeliers when someone gets the Holy Ghost. But when it comes to emotional problems, "Oh, just trust the Lord, brother." Or we seek to counsel people from human reasoning and not the revealed truths of the Spirit. Let me tell you some-thing; it takes more than just getting the Holy Ghost and speaking in tongues to have your emotions healed. You can operate in a gift but never come to truly know the giver of the gift, resting in His love and still live daily in defeat from condemnation. I know how it feels to see blind eyes opened, deaf ears unstopped and even the dead raised but, battle daily with discouragement and defeat in my life from not walking in the Spirit-intimacy with Christ.

I've had the Holy Spirit for many years, and I'm just now getting healing for things that happened decades ago. This healing is simply coming as a result of walking in the revelation of His word, both Rhema (spoken) and Logos (written) and daily resting in His love and peace through intimacy. You can pray and fast – and I suppose I've done as much as some – but you have to go back where you missed a turn and rest in His innocence, rest in His Righteousness. 2 Corinthians 4:7 records; "However, we possess this precious treasure [the divine Light of the Gospel] in [frail, human] vessels of earth, that the grandeur and exceeding greatness of the power may be shown to be from God and not from ourselves." (AMP)

You must realize that you're not damaged goods. It doesn't matter how much you were abused, you're not a dirty vessel. You are a vessel of Honor, fit for the Masters use (2 Timothy 2:21)! It doesn't matter how much was done to you, Jesus can take it away. Let God touch you right now. Pray this prayer:

"Lord, I receive your innocence. I receive your purity. I rest in your love, simply because I am your son/daughter. I don't have to jump through hoops and climb ladders to be approved

117

of you and receive your love. Thank you for taking away my impurity and giving me your innocence through to power of your blood. I receive your innocence. I refuse to blame myself for things beyond my control. I will not hold myself emotionally hostage for events that were beyond my control. I will not hold a grudge against myself for poor choices I have made. My parents' divorce was not my fault. The abuse I suffered was not what I deserved. I receive the peace of God right now. I claim your innocence, In Jesus Name!"

That is how quickly it is done. Right now thousands of pounds of mental anguish and guilt have been cut loose from you. Begin to praise Him. Worship Him for His holiness. Praise Him for your deliverance.

Stop holding yourself hostage. Some of us have prayed hours, but our prayers have been hindered because we were trying to do penance. We fasted to punish ourselves, and it has not been in faith. God has honored it, but He wants to release us into a higher dimension of liberty and faith. Your fasting is going to be with faith; your prayers are going to be with faith. Your fasting and prayer will now cause you to mount up with wings of an eagle and fly with Him in heavenly places (Isaiah 40:31, Ephesians 2:6).Walk in liberty

118

son and daughter of God. Walk in authority. Walk in the supernatural covering of His presence. You are free.

Endnotes

[iii] Biblesoft's New Exhaustive Strong's Numbers and Concordance with Expanded Greek-Hebrew Dictionary. Copyright © 1994, 2003, 2006 Biblesoft, Inc. and International Bible Translators, Inc.

[ii] Ibid

[iii] NT:1342 dikaios (dik'-ah-yos); from NT:1349; equitable (in character or act); by implication, innocent, holy (absolutely or relatively):(Biblesoft's New Exhaustive Strong's Numbers and Concordance with Expanded Greek-Hebrew Dictionary. Copyright © 1994, 2003, 2006 Biblesoft, Inc. and International Bible Translators, Inc.)

[iv] from Adam Clarke's Commentary, Electronic Database. Copyright © 1996, 2003, 2005, 2006 by Biblesoft, Inc. All rights reserved.

[v] NT:38Biblesoft's New Exhaustive Strong's Numbers and Concordance with Expanded Greek-Hebrew Dictionary. Copyright © 1994, 2003, 2006 Biblesoft, Inc. and International Bible Translators, Inc.

5
Personal Testimony

As we discussed earlier, Joseph of the Old Testament named his first child Manasseh, which means "to forget.[i]" When Joseph chose to forget the betrayal and wounding from his brethren, then the second revival came – the second son born – Ephraim – "double blessing.[ii]" When you choose to release, forget, and give it to God, then you become a candidate for the double blessing from the Lord. I'm writing for people who are sitting right now in prisons of bitterness. What was done to you was not right. What you went through was horrible. I am not going to disrespect you by downplaying the reality of your hurt and disappointment. You look at other people and say, "Oh, if I could have that name, been raised in *that* home environment, if I could be involved in that ministry. Oh, if I could have those finances or that staff, if I just had the breaks, I could really do things . . ." Let me tell you something, my friend, if you'll find a place with God and get a hold of Him with desperation, God can break the chains of whatever it is that has happened in your life and can cause a beauty, power, and glory to come forth from the brokenness, wounding and humiliation. God can make you bloom where you are planted and bring forth much fruit for His glory. Heritage will never get you what hunger must. Heritage will never do for you what hunger, passion, intimacy, and desire with Jesus will do! When we set our hearts to pursue Him, we will find Him!

God spoke of this principle in Jeremiah to those who He allowed to be sold into captivity that they might return to pursuit of Him, Jeremiah 29:11-14 "For I know the thoughts and plans that I have for you, says the Lord, thoughts and plans for welfare and peace and not for evil, to give you hope in your final outcome. 12 Then you will call upon Me, and you will come and pray to Me, and I will hear and heed you. 13 Then you will seek Me, inquire for, and require Me [as a vital necessity] and find Me when you search for Me with all your heart. 14 I will be found by you, says the Lord, and I will release you from captivity and gather you from all the nations and all the places to which I have driven you, says the Lord, and I will bring you back to the place from which I caused you to be carried away captive." (AMP)

You can sit there and lament your situation and say, "I've had all the wrong breaks – I've been dealt a lemon in life." Or you can rise up and become a dreamer. When God truly turns us from the captivities of our past then we will become dreamers. Psalms 126:1states; "When the Lord turned again the captivity of Zion, we were like them that dream." The word *dream* in this verses is derives from the Hebrew word *chalam* (khaw-lam'); a primitive root; properly, to bind firmly, i.e. (by implication) to be (causatively to make) plump; also (through the figurative sense of dumbness) to dream:[iii]

Dreamers use the strengths of the pain and failures to drive themselves to the cross and closer to Jesus to release the full potential of God's will and purpose. There is a huge difference between having a dream and being a dreamer. Joseph has a dream but after 13 years in the prison of his trial he transformed to being a dreamer (Genesis 37-42). He became inseparately fused to his dream. He became the dream fulfilled. That's why, when you're a dreamer, my friend, you don't just have a dream in your hand. That thing has become fused with who you are; you won't just walk away from it. You won't just sell out for some thrill in the back seat of a car or a cheap hotel room. You won't just sell out for some illicit relationship or a drug or alcohol. Why? I know, as I'm a dreamer.

Too many people approach the word of God as a rule book. They strive to gain the approval of God by "keeping the law." Jesus desires to transform our appetites that we will desire the things of His Spirit, not this world. This is why he said in John 14:15, "If you [really] love Me, you will keep (obey) My commands." (AMP) It is our passionate pursuit of Him that transforms our spiritual appetites and causes us to desire to please Him. Those who fall in love with Jesus, have no problem shunning the world and keeping His commandments.

I've paid a price for this anointing. I've wept many nights. I haven't come this far to throw everything away for something dumb or something temporal. Oh, if you just have a dream in your hand, and it gets tough and someone talks bad about you, you'll put it aside, and you'll go and have a pity party and give up on the dream. When you're a dreamer, you may get tired, you may get weary, and you may go through times when you'll question everything in life. You may even wonder if God knows where you're at. But when you go to hang your dream up, there will be a ripping, there'll be a tearing, there'll be a pulling, and you won't be able to walk away. Why? You're a dreamer. That thing has become who you are. It's fused to you. I won't walk away, I can't sell out, I wont' give in! I must hold on, because I am a dreamer.

My Beginning

On July tenth of 1965, I was born into a broken home. My birth father desired and endeavored to become a scientist. My mother worked as a dancer in a topless bar in El Paso, Texas. When my father learned that she was being unfaithful to him, he moved out never to reenter our lives. She then had to care for my older brother, older sister, and me on her own, which proved to be more of a responsibility than she wanted at the time.

I was only two months old when my young mother decided she could not cope with the responsibility of children and live the kind of life she wanted as well. She hired a babysitter to watch us in our apartment in El Paso promising to return home by seven-thirty that evening. Instead, she climbed into her car and began the two-thousand-mile drive to Florida where her father lived. She left in good faith that the babysitter would turn us over to the authorities once she realized that my mother had abandoned us. Logically the department of family services would take us into custody, find us a good home, and thus end her "problems."

Unfortunately, she didn't realize that the baby-sitter, being from Mexico, didn't have the legal right to work or reside in the United States. She had to get across the border before dark or she would be fined. So, expecting my mother to be home any time, she left us in the apartment. She closed the door, locked it, and left. For many days we lived with no care, food, or water.

Approximately 10 days later, the manager came and checked the apartment to see if Mother had moved out. When he found us, he called the authorities, who brought in paramedics as well. They said I wouldn't live because my kidneys were failing and my skin had turned yellow with poison and toxins. They transported me to the hospital via a life-flight helicopter. The medical professionals employed machines to breath for me and sustain my vital functions. Day after day I laid there while they said, "This baby will never make it. If he does make it, he'll be a vegetable with no liver or kidney functions."

My paternal Grandparents lived a very simple, poor life on the Mescalero Apache Indian Reservation in Carrizozo, New Mexico. When my grandparents found out that I was dying in the hospital, they came down immediately. Every day for several months they drove the ninety miles to be with me and in their simple faith, pray over me. My grandfather, although he wasn't spirit filled, was full of love. He said, "I don't care how much it costs or what it takes; this child's going to make it." With time, God miraculously raised me from that intensive care unit. God had plans for that helpless baby!

Today the devil will come around saying, "I'm gonna' do this . . ., I'm gonna' kill you, I'm gonna' take your family," or whatever. I simply reply, "You know what, devil? You couldn't kill me when I was two months old. What makes you think you can kill me now?" Let me tell you, when you have a destiny in God, there is not a devil in hell big enough to stop you. There's not a problem big enough. There's not a situation bad enough!

My grandparents raised us for about three and a half years. Meanwhile, my mother remarried. This man had no idea that she had any children. One day she finally revealed to him that she had three children she just couldn't just forget about. She took the issue to court, and, after a long battle and a miracle, all charges were eventually dropped against my mother, and she won us back. I want to boldly give her honor for making a great effort to be a good mother ever since then. I give her honor for taking care of us, and I don't want to dishonor her in any way in the telling of this story. My pure desire is to give those who face broken pasts hope. We moved to Northern Connecticut.

When I was six years old, while our family was living in northern Connecticut, someone came and knocked on the door and handed my parents a tract inviting them to a Pentecostal service. My mother went that same weekend, and God filled her with His Spirit. A year later, God filled my stepfather with the Holy Spirit as well. Only a year and a half afterwards, God began to move on him with a call to preach. They moved to Austin, Texas, and began to attend Westgate Apostolic Church. There he began assisting Pastor Jimmy Jones. My Mother became involved in the Deaf Ministry.

Baptized in His Name

At nine years old, God wondrously filled me with His Spirit, and I was baptized in the wonderful Name of Jesus. My whole life was wrapped around commitment to the work of God, street services, all-night prayer meetings, church services, and revivals ect... When I was eleven years old, I remember Brother Charles Mahaney preaching a message during the Junior Crusader Youth Camp that moved me deeply. He delivered a sermon about the King's Anointing on a Shepherd Boy's Life, and it caused me to fall down weeping and crying on the floor of that campground. Late that night the dorm counselors came to me, shaking me. I don't know how long I had been lost in the presence of God. They said, "Son, you have to go back to your dorm; it's 'lights out' time." God was calling me to preach, and I knew it.

About that same time, things began to fall apart in our home. My stepfather, who by now was an ordained preacher, began to physically and mentally/emotionally abuse us children, not sexually, but he would beat us quite often and work us over pretty bad. Rejection began to rule in our home. Many times I remember giving him Father's Day cards only for him to hand them back to me saying, "I'm sorry, but I'm not your dad." Still, I remained committed to God. I brought my bible with me each day to school, all the way up to my senior year in High School, sharing Christ with all who would let me. I would take long walks, praying and asking God to deliver me from this living hell.

When I was sixteen years old, he beat me so severely in the garage that my Mother tried to come in, begging him to stop. He turned and snarled, get out of here or your next. At age eighteen, I knew I had to leave because I had returned home early one afternoon from school and heard the muffled cries of my sister coming from her room. I look thru the partly open door and discovered my stepfather raping my sister with a butcher knife to her throat. He had been doing this for over 5 years. He threatened to kill her if she told anyone. I remember the day I walked out of the house with my clothes in a little garbage bag, and I walked away full of anger, bound by bitterness. For a year I ran from God. I said, "I'll never be a preacher. I don't want anything to do with that! If that's what it means to be a preacher, God, I don't care if you have called me, I'll never do it." I ran and I ran.

After about a year, I went to college and decided to be a structural steel engineer. Because I wanted to make something of my life, I threw myself into it. I worked while trying to go to school. I was just trying to make something out of my broken existence. It was the mercy of God that kept me from the drugs and alcohol scene. Other than being promiscuous, I focused all my time on achieving. During that winter my health broke, and I became very sick with double pneumonia. As I lay on the couch, sick with a high temperature, God got my attention. I have a divine visitor that entered that room that night. God knows just how to put you flat on your back so He can talk to you.

It was as if God was saying, "No way, son, you've prayed too many prayers! You committed your heart to me years ago. You said you'd do it for me, and I'll never let you go. I won't let you just go out and destroy your life. I have plans for you. I'm going to do something in your life."

This divine visitor began to converse with me asking, "Why do you blame God for His creation's mistakes? You know the only love you can find is in the house of God."

As I lay there, I began to weep and cry and said, "I can't forgive them! I can never face them again." "I absolutely hate my stepfather."

I remember that voice saying, "If you'll just try, I'll help you through it."

It had been about a year and a half since I'd prayed. I hadn't even talked to God. I slipped my hands in the air and said, "Jesus, are you still there?" Instantly, the love of God flooded that room! It felt as If my Father reached down and just wrapped His arms of love and compassion around me. It had been over 1 ½ years since I had felt that kind of love.

That Sunday I went and found the church in Round Rock, Texas. My parents had helped the pastor start that church. We had helped them put chairs out each week as they began that Home Missions church. I walked into the Sunday morning service and didn't even wait for the preaching to finish. I ran to the the altar right then and there and gave my heart back to the Lord. I threw myself on that altar and gave myself back over to God, lock, stock, and barrel. I said, "Lord Jesus, I will never leave you, I will never ever again turn my back on you." I can truly say, that by the grace of God, I have been discouraged from time to time, but I have never contemplated leaving Him again.

The Hurts Continue

I wish I could tell you that things just turned right around. Instead, they spiraled down even further. I had worked hard to acquire a nice sports car, nice clothes and living a nice lifestyle. Within one year, I lost them all. I believe my resolve to serve the Lord; no matter what came my way was being tested. I simply gave myself over to just praying and fasting, seeking desperately to know God in a deeper manner. I also focused daily on winning souls to God. After a few months I found myself driven to spend weeks fasting and focused prayer for different seasons. Why? Because there so much pain and hurt locked up in my spirit, my only hope was my passionate pursuit of Him. What had happened in our home finally surfaced. My stepfather turned his ministerial license in, and my mother and he divorced. Everything went to shambles. It had such an impact on my brother that, to this day, he is mentally handicapped and still lives with my Mother. Just to see the family disintegrate can do that to a person. That's the horror of what sin can do.

About the end of 1985, I just stayed involved in the church by seeking the face of the Lord daily and winning souls. I wouldn't go to camp meetings and other such events because people would come around prying for information about my stepfather. I got tired of talking about it. Anytime the subject would come up, I felt incredible shame. Instead, I just wanted to close myself in with God and continue reaching the lost. In the midst of my pain and hurt, I just tried to find my way closer to Him. One day, after a 21 day period of fasting and prayer, God spoke to me and said, "I want you to move to Houston, Texas. There I will heal you and release the ministry I have for you." At the time, I did not even know one person who lived in Houston, Texas. Nevertheless, in complete obedience to the leading of the Spirit, I sold what things I had and left with my pastor's blessings. I had just enough money to purchase a Greyhound Bus ticket. I could not afford a suitcase, so I placed my clothes and be-longings in a Hefty® garbage bag.

I left Austin intending to go to Bible College, al-though I didn't have the funds for it yet. An official with the school had written me a letter that said, "Go ahead and come anyway with what you have, we will help you get a job and get started with your bible col-lege courses" I bought the Greyhound bus ticket, which left me with seventy-five dollars in my wallet. My luggage consisted of a trumpet and a Hefty® gar-bage bag with all my clothes. When I got off the bus in downtown Houston, it was a Thursday afternoon. I remember looking up at those skyscrapers thinking, *What am I doing here? I felt so completely all alone.*

I then caught the city bus down to Broadway Street and arrived on the college campus. As I walked toward the office, the administrator with whom I'd been in communication came walking toward me shaking his head with tears running down his face. He said, "I'm sorry, Brother Arcovio." I looked him, won-dering, "What is he talking about." I was shortly going to find out.

Behind him came walking a leading official of that college with a terrible frown on his face. Up to this date I had never met such a vicious religious spirit. He walked up to me and said, "Aren't you John Arcovio?"

I said, "Yes."

He said, "Wasn't your dad Ray Arcovio?"

"Yes, sir."

"Didn't your dad molest and rape your sister?"

"Yes, he did . . ." I searched the men's faces. "But that doesn't have anything to do with me."

He said, "Oh yes it does! The apple doesn't fall far from the tree. You'll never be a preacher with the name Arcovio, son. Your name is mud. Just go back where you came from. You go back. You may be able to teach Bible studies and help in your local church, but you'll never be a preacher." (Don't' ever underestimate the power of a religious spirit. It was religious spirit's that killed Jesus.)

Let me warn you – if you listen to what life tells you, you'll never amount to anything. If you listen to what people tell you, despair will keep you down. When God has spoken to you in the brightness of His revelation word, you must hold onto that in the midnight hour when it seems every spirit from hell is trying to destroy your walk and calling from God.

This is why Paul instructed his son in the gospel, Timothy in 1 Timothy 1:18, "This charge I commit unto thee, son Timothy, according to the prophecies which went before on thee, that thou by them mightest war a good warfare;"

You've got to believe that if God has called you, if God has touched you, if God has said, "I'll do it," then He will do it! There will come a time when no one will believe it but you. Many people will tell you they believe in you when the vision is accomplished and they see the finished result of the fire. Very few will truly believe in you, "before you get there." Your complete trust and faith must be in God and the word he has spoken to you. You've got to get a hold of something from God and believe that He will do it.

I got back on a bus and thought, *Where am I going to go?* I didn't have enough money to move back to Austin. I only had enough money for food, transportation and lodging for about three days. As I rode down Broadway Street at about 8:30 on a Thursday evening, tears streamed down my face. I was crushed. It seemed as though my dream was dead. I'd never been treated that way by anybody. It would be many years before I understood the principle of wounding that God allows for my better. We face our greatest wounds, not from enemies but from the house of God. This was the lament of King David in Psalms 55:12-14, "For it is not an enemy who reproaches and taunts me — then I might bear it; nor is it one who has hated me who insolently vaunts himself against me — then I might hide from him. 13 But it was you, a man my equal, my companion and my familiar friend. 14 We had sweet fellowship together and used to walk to the house of God in company. (AMP)

It is also recorded in Zechariah 13:6, "And one shall say unto him, What are these wounds in thine hands? Then he shall answer, Those with which I was wounded in the house of my friends." We should not be surprised when God allows brethren to wound us deeply, God often allows this to produce the sweet fragrance of His Holy anointing oil in our lives. The greater the intensity of the fire, the greater the joy and reward. Pau wrote of this in 1 Peter 4:12-13, "Beloved, think it not strange concerning the fiery trial which is to try you, as though some strange thing happened unto you:13 But rejoice, inasmuch as ye are partakers of Christ's sufferings; that, when his glory shall be revealed, ye may be glad also with exceeding joy."

I said, "God, I thought I heard your voice. I thought you told me to come here. I have nowhere to go." As I watched out the bus window, I saw a sign that said Life Tabernacle United Pentecostal Church. God spoke to me and said, "Stop and get off here; this is where I'm going to heal you."

The Healing Begins

I reached up and hit the button to stop the bus. I climbed down from that vehicle and walked into a church foyer with beautiful marble floors. I'd never seen a church so beautiful. I found a corner to set my little trumpet and bag of clothes down. I entered in the middle of the church service, and Bro. Phillips, the usher, stopped me and said, "I'm sorry, son, church is in progress. You'll have to sit in the back."

I said, "Oh sir, I've never sat anywhere but in the front row."

He looked at me for a moment, studying my face. "Well, son, if you want to sit in the front, then you're going to sit in the front," he condescended. He took me all the way down, and I was able to find a place on the second row.

As I sat down, suddenly a cocoon of the love and Spirit and power of God began to minister to me, and God said, "Welcome home, son. Now I'm going to do something in your life!" I became lost in love and worship for my savior, completely forgetting I was sitting in a church with 1,600 members.

In a church the saints must be sensitive. You don't know who's going to walk through those back doors. You don't know where they have come from. You don't know what God has in store for that individual. A church is to be a haven of love. It must be a

138

house of healing, a home of comfort, and a place of mercy. There with the healing power of His presence, God will fulfill His destiny in someone's broken life. According to some, I don't belong in God's kingdom. I should be somewhere broken, hopeless, an outcast. God has been good to me. He has saved and kept me by His grace, lifting me to where I am today in Him. You have no excuse – if God can do it for me, He can do it for you.

There in Houston I found a job. A man offered to let me spray oil spots off the parking spaces of expensive condos. My pay was that I got to sleep on the concrete floor of his little warehouse just off Interstate 45. Once a day He'd take me to a fast food restaurant to buy me a meal. For three months I worked in the Texas heat spraying those spots with muriatic acid. The acid would eat holes in all of my clothes I wore to work in. I'd say, "God, I've given you everything. I'm just trying to follow you. I know you've called me." I never lost hope that God was going to bring me through. We must never allow ourselves to lose hope, no matter what we go through in life. A man can live about 40 days without food, about 9 days without water, about 8 minutes without air but he cannot live one second without hope. I'd go back to that warehouse and lay on the oil-stained floor in the evening heat and listen to the traffic go by. The devil would laugh at me and say, "Great 'call of God' you've got, son. Great preacher *you* are. Look at you. You're almost homeless. Nobody loves you – God doesn't even love you."

My friend, if you let Him, God will get you where you can trust Him. Where you have to trust Him. Many times I would walk into the church and give the whole night to talking to Jesus. Sometimes I spent the whole night praying and talking to Jesus. Somewhere around three or four in the morning the pain would lift. The hurts of my past would be eased. He would free me from my anguish. It was during those times that I would just bask in His love and embrace, never wanting to leave.

One evening, I lay down in my sleeping bag on the concrete warehouse just off Monroe Blvd and Interstate 45 but on that particular night, I could not sleep. Suddenly I sensed an awful darkness fill the warehouse and I literally felt hands pressing my chest to the ground. I could hardly breathe and I could hear thousands of voices like the buzzing of bees. They were shouting insult, taunts and threats like, "Look at you, you're a homeless loser." "You are some great preacher, look what all your fasting, prayer and sacrifice has gotten you, nothing." "Nobody loves you or even cares if you are alive, just commit suicide." I struggled to

140

move but could not. I felt completely helpless under this demonic attack. Finally I began to think, "Jesus." Each time I would think His name, the buzzing voices would retreat a little and the force pressing my chest to the floor would subside. I kept thinking, "Jesus, Jesus, Jesus." Then I sat up and screamed, "In Jesus Name!" The voices and presence retreated to a spot a little ways from when I was laying. I stood up, shaking from head to toe but pointed into the demonic manifestation and say, 'You are right devil, I am nobody. You have stripped me of everything, my family, and possessions. You can even strip me down to the clothes I have on my body, but you will NEVER take my call of God and love for my savior! I am called of God and I WILL PREACH ON DAY! You just wait and see!" In a flash the darkness and buzzing voices left. I felt absolutely victorious until later that afternoon when the man who was employing me informed me that he had no more work for me and I had to move out of the warehouse immediately. I checked my funds and I had $40. I rented a room at the YMCA across the interstate from where Life Tabernacle Church was located. The room was $17.50 a week and had one cot, one small stand in the room. I had to take my showers in a large communal room. Mostly drug addicts, alcoholics and homeless people stayed there. I immediately began scouring the newspaper for another job as I only had enough money to survive another week or so. I searched for five days to no avail.

One morning I went to the church and just sat down on the front pew. I had a long list of different jobs I could go and check on. About two months earlier a classified help wanted ad from a company called Whirlwind Steel Buildings had caught my interest because I had a little bit of training from my college days in architectural drafting. I had applied but inadvertently supplied an incorrect phone number for the church I was attending as my contact number. I was just sitting there reading my bible when the back door opened and down the aisle came Pastor James Kilgore. He walked up and said, "Well hello, Brother Johnny!" I didn't even know he knew my name. This was the first time he ever spoke to me. Unknown to me, he knew the first day I attended the services and knew who my parents were and my story. However, the Lord had instructed him in prayer to leave me alone and simply watch me. He'd been watching me, praying for me for the past four months. He said, "How's it going?"

"All right, I'm just trying to find another job and place to stay" I said.

He said, "Brother Johnny, I want you to just do what is in your heart. Forget about the Bible college

thing; there are better circumstances coming for you."
"You just make Life Tabernacle here your bible college
and God will use you some day." He then turned and
left. I immediately felt the Spirit prompt me to return
to Whirlwind Steel Buildings.

I put my best slacks and white shirt with a tie
that I had and went to Whirlwind Steel Buildings.
When I walked through the front doors and introduced
myself to the receptionist she stopped what she was
doing and looked at me saying, "John Arcovio! We have
been trying to call you for four weeks." She then said,
"Wait here." She went into the back and brought the
head draftsman forward. He looked and me and said,
"Are you John Arcovio?" I replied , "Yes, Sir." He then
said, "would you like this job?" I exuberantly replied,
"Yes, Sir!" He then said, "When can you start." I replied
"How about right now!" He had me first take a drug
test then they hired me as a draftsman, sight unseen,
giving me a tremendous amount of starting pay for a
young man. My life began to get a little better. I pulled
a broke 1969 Chevy Handi Van from a junkyard called
Pick-Y-Parts. With the help of a sweet old man who
was a mechanic in Life Tabernacle, he helped me drop
a 1972 Dodge Comet engine in this van. Only three of
the motor mount bolts lines up and it ran hot, burning
oil every day, but, man, I finally had wheels again! I

continued to give myself over to praying, fasting, and winning souls. I took the little van and built some wood benches in it. Since the church didn't have a bus ministry at that time, I just went out in the neighborhood knocking on doors and asking, "Do you mind if I take your children to church?" I would fill that van with twenty-thirty children each Sunday, making two to three trips. One summer God filled over fifty children with His Spirit! I began teaching Bible studies to the parents, and revival began to break forth. I witnessed several families come to God through that ministry. Then I started going o the University of Houston College campus with a friend Jerry Samouse. We would teach a bible class on the campus after hours. We started having revival at the University of Houston with people being filled with His Spirit. We started baptizing 20-30 students at a time in the huge water fountain out front of the dormitories. There are missionaries overseas doing the work of God today as a result of this revival.

My Preaching Ministry Begins

After some time of sitting and healing under Brother Kilgore – ministering in the altar, working in children's church, picking up kids, teaching bible classes at the college, soul-winning, soul-winning,

soul-winning – God began a new work in me. You cannot go wrong if you fall in love with Jesus and fall in
love with souls.

By the summer of 1988, I had preached a total
of four times. I had four little messages I had preaced
in children's church, which were pathetic in retros-
pect. Two of them God gave me in a dream. Twice in a
dream I'm standing in a pulpit, and an invisible hand
is turning pages. I would wake up and get my Bible,
which I slept with, and write the message down. One
sermon was called "From The Anointing to the Shekinah." The other, a message about His Spirit, consisted
of setting up a line of little cups in front of the congregation. I would preach about fifteen minutes on the
story of the widow (2 Kings 4:1-7) and say, "Just like
God can fill these cups with oil, He can fill you with
His Spirit. Now who wants His Spirit?" In the simple
setting of children's church, God would fill twenty with
His Spirit.

One night, during a time of 21 days of prayer
and fasting, the Lord spoke to me and said, "I want
you to go full time in the ministry."

"Full time? A full-time evangelist?" The four
times I had preached were just in children's church.
Now God was telling me to begin preaching in
churches to adults. I was scared. I was very, very sa-

tisfied with just being there in the church, loving Jesus, winning souls and serving my pastor. Finally I walked up to Brother Kilgore trembling and nervous and stammered, "Uh, I don't want to be out of order, sir, but God has spoken to me to go full time in the ministry." I cringed, waiting for his rebuke; instead, he completely shocked me.

He smiled, put his arm on my shoulder, and said, "You've heard from God, son. Just be careful." Then he walked off. I had hoped he would call somebody and get me a place to preach. I knew God had called me to preach way back when I was about twelve years old. I was twenty-four when I finally preached my first message. God puts you through the fire for a reason, my friend. I got a little truck with a camper on the back of it, threw a mattress in there with a sleeping bag, paid what bills I had, jumped in my truck, and took off. After driving about 2 hours I pulled into a rest stop as I realized, I did not even know where I was going! I figured I'd better pray and ask Him where to go. After about an hour of praying in tongues, God told me to head for West Texas. I got out my map and found the road leading into the west part of Texas. On my way I stopped as the Lord directed and preached for a few small churches. Most of the pastors just shook my hand after I was finished and thanked me for stopping by and preaching for their church, but no offering was given. Son I was down to about $120 for gas and food. I slept in the back of my truck and bought cans of soup to make the funds stretch. Many nights I prayed the whle night, just seeking the face of God.

I was trying to find God and His direction. I would stay in state parks three days to a week at a time, just fasting and praying. "God, where do you want me to preach now?" I would ask. He would lead me to the next small church to preach at. I had one suit to my name that Brother Kilgore had given me. It was too big for me. I kept the pants all bunched up in the back with a huge safety pin. I'd preach and pull the coat off, and people would just stare thinking I was from another world. I kept my hair slicked straight back and wore huge horn-rimmed glasses – I looked wild! I'm surprised anybody allowed me to preach. When I look at some of those old tapes and videos of my preaching, I just cringe. Boy, I was a sight for sore eyes.

God used me because I was sold out to Him. I was not fasting and praying for anything, I was fasting and praying to know him in a deeper manner. God knew if He'd say it to me, I'd say it to the people. If He told me to do something, I would do it. I loved Him with all my heart. I loved souls. There were nights I'd lay in that truck in twenty-degree weather just praising God out loud like I had no sense. The devil would laugh and say, "Yeah, look at your great ministry." But I just ignored Him and keep praying and seeking the face of God. I fasted and prayed so much in those days, my clothes just hung on my body like a rag dolls, but I held onto my dream! My friend, hang on; dreams don't die when God gives them. I just had to hang on.

God has given me a wonderful wife and beautiful children. God has opened so many doors across the world to our ministry. So many pastors have been so kind to us. So many things have happened. I remember when I met my wife's relatives. My wife comes from a wonderful heritage, and I honor her heritage – not that it entitles her to greatness, but she has a great lineage to draw from.

Once I pulled into a certain town and was almost out of gas. I was on my way to a meeting that God had opened for me in New Mexico. I thought, *Well, I'm going to call the pastor and see if I can park my truck on his church parking lot. We'll see what happens tomorrow.* It was eleven-thirty at night when I called and said, "Hello Pastor Taylor, this is John Arcovio. I'm an evangelist from Houston, Texas. I am driving to New Mexico for a meeting I am going to preach. Could I park my truck on your parking lot tonight and rest, I have a camper built in it?"

"Brother, it's getting down to ten degrees."

"It's okay; I've got a sleeping bag." What he didn't know was that I had just spent four days in a campground forty miles out of town, I knew how cold it got each evening. I spent the time praying and fasting – not that I was super spiritual – I just didn't have any food or place to preach. He replied, " No brother, come to my house and stay the night." He next day was Sunday. He let me stay and preach that morning and evening service and revival broke out for 9 weeks. I eventually got to New Mexico about 10 months later to preach for the original pastor who has invited me. That was the first break I got in a revival. I preached for him every year after that meeting and we had some glorious moves of the Spirit. I started getting invitations from churches in the area weekly after that meeting. From there, in that area-wide revival, I believe I preached 128 services in a row without a break. Hundreds of souls were filled with God's Spirit during that time. I'd close on a Sunday night, and someone would call and say, "Can you be here Monday night?" Dreams don't die! God was fulfilling what He'd promised me He would do.

Going back over this, it has been difficult for me to share my past, but I want to give someone hope. I want you to know that you, too, can make it and overcome.

God Gives a Vision

Prior to entering the ministry I had an experience in 1987 back in Houston. One night I was at the church praying under the very back pew as I often did. I lay there talking to God, pouring out my heart saying, "God, I just want to be used by you. I have nothing to offer to you, but you can come and use me. I give myself to you, although I feel I have nothing to give you. Here I am, Lord, use me for your service and Glory." Little did I realize, I had all he needed, my heart. All He wants is your heart, my friend. A while later I began to weep and travail in prayer. Suddenly I was no longer in that sanctuary in Life Tabernacle. I was standing in a huge wooden pulpit preaching a message about the delivering power of the Name of Jesus. In the vision, God's Spirit swept over a crowd of several hundred of thousands of people like a hurricane healing and delivering them. The next thing I knew, I was back in the church praying again. I couldn't tell anyone that – after all, I was just a Sunday school teacher and a children's minister. I just put that vision in my heart and held onto it.

Several years later, in 1994, I was invited to go to the country of Ethiopia as an intercessor. I went only to pray – just to be a fly on the wall. I was so excited to be able to physically experience the greatest revival in the history of that nation. On our way to the service on Friday night, the Ethiopians' hunger for God and their fervency moved me strongly. As we pulled up to the open field where they were conducting the crusade, which consisted of an open cow field, a line of choir members were leaping and shouting as they praised and worshipped God. I was weeping and groaning because of the burden of the Spirit of the Lord when suddenly Brother Teklemariam stood up and said "Brethren, God has spoken to me that Brother Arcovio has the message for tonight."

Somewhere in the back of my consciousness I heard 'Arcovio,' and worry and fear crawled into my mind. Something started flipping in my stomach, just dancing and kicking. Thank God I had thought to bring my Bible! I wondered, *Lord, why didn't you tell me this? God, what am I going to say?* There were national church leaders from the USA at that meeting – men far greater than I was. There were four-hundred-thousand plus people aiting in the crowd to receive the word from the man of God – many with a relationship with God far greater than I'll ever dream of. I had five minutes from the time we got off the bus to the time we walked into the conference center to find the mind of God. That was the longest walk I ever took in my life. I walked as slowly as I could. God didn't say anything. I was sitting there flipping through my Bible thinking, *Oh, Jesus! What am I going to preach? I could not even think to quote one scripture, my mind was blank.*

I sat there on the platform and all too soon they sang and finished the songs. I'm sitting there saying, "God, what am I going to do?" Finally Teklemariam turns and says, "Okay, we are ready. Come!" Things began to go blurry, and everything went in slow motion as I began to walk towards that platform. In my mind, I saw myself ten years earlier as a young man praying under a pew, and suddenly the scenario fit – the pulpit and the crowd of thousands. I said to myself, "Hey, I recognize that wooden pulpit. I recognize this crowd of people." Instantly I knew what I was going to preach- "The Delivering Power of the Name, Jesus.". I opened my Bible, and for fifteen minutes I shared a message about the delivering power of the Name of Jesus. I couldn't finish my delivery because God hit that place, just like He had shown in the dream, with hurricane for winds of the Spirit! I fell on my face on that platform as thousands were delivered by His powerful Name!

That same power of Jesus is with you right now to deliver you if you'll let him. He will heal you if you will let the past go. Just let it go. Dreams won't die when God gives them.

Learning to Forgive

The hardest thing I ever did was to pick up the phone that day and call my stepfather. He didn't want anything to do with us – ever. I said, "Ray, I love you. I forgive you for everything that ever happened." Even with his negative, mocking, rejecting response, I chose to forgive and I released him, because God had told me, "You'll never go any higher until you get this out of your heart. You must forgive and forget." I would not be where I am in Christ today if I had not chosen to forgive and forget.

How do I know I'm over it? Because, when I think about it, it's just a memory – there's no pain in my heart. I can tell these accounts simply as facts; the searing pain that used to be attached to the stories is gone, healed by the blood of the lamb. If there's still pain, you haven't forgiven. When you forgive and forget, God will heal it. It'll just be a memory. You won't be ashamed about it. You won't hang your head; you'll realize what a miracle God has performed. You will realize what a trophy of the grace of God you are.

Some of you have been carrying weights and chains all these years, but God wants you to be free. God wants to do something awesome in your situation. Your pain will leave. Your dilemma is not your destiny! This trial will not destroy you, but rather develop you into the vessel of His making. You're going to be free from what your dad did to you. You're going to be free from what your uncle or other family member did to you. Whoever it was that has wounded you, you will overcome it! You're going to be free from the memories, the pain, the weight, and the bitterness. You can be loosed right now. Anger will lift. Discouragement and depression are going to lift off your shoulders. You're going to be transformed. You must believe it!

Let me just show you what my Jesus does. In 1996, Brother Billy Cole asked me to go and be a part of the team that was doing the crusade called the Houston Summit. I recall that over a thousand people received His Spirit in that crusade. I hadn't been back to Houston in several years since venturing out in my little truck In 1988 following the voice and call of God. I was now married with children and flying around the world preaching every week somewhere. I flew in and a young man from the church picked us up informing us, "I'm going to be taking you to your hotel." Suddenly I realized we were going down Interstate 45 toward the area of the warehouse where I used to sleep. I turned to Brother Cole and, with great excitement, said, "Brother Cole, remember that story I told you about that little warehouse? It's just right off this highway."

To my amazement, we got off on the same exit I knew so well and began going down the same access road, Monroe Boulevard. My heart began to pound – I hadn't been back in seven years, and we were going to pass right by the warehouse. I leaned over to the young man driving and said, "Sir, could you stop for just five minutes? I want to show Brother Cole a location. Right around this bend you're going to see this old dilapidated warehouse." We rounded the bend, but there was no warehouse! They had torn it down and built a five-star Marriot Hotel.

To my further amazement, our car pulled up to the hotel, and our driver said, "This is where you are staying."

I may laugh when thinking about it now, but I wasn't laughing then, I was deeply moved to tears. I checked into my room, set my luggage down, and then slipped out the back door. I walked out onto the parking lot in that dark night and fell to my knees on the pavement. I wept and cried out saying, "Jesus, only you could take young man sleeping on a cold concrete floor right on this very spot – a young man thinking his life was over – and bring him back twelve years later and put him on a king-size bed. Only you can do that Jesus, only you!"

Get ready, my friend, God wants to do something for you! Your miracle breakthrough is coming. Just stay faithful to God. I want to pray a prayer of deliverance over you right now;

By the power of the Name of Jesus, by the authority of the Word of God, I rebuke depression, bitterness, and spirits of oppression, failure, and shame in Jesus Name. I loose you into your destiny! I command every spirit that would try to torment and drive you to be broken, in Jesus Name! I release the destiny of the Spirit in your life. In Jesus Name! Amen!

Lift your voice and claim His destiny for you. Speak with tongues and strengthen your inner man. Let God heal you! Dreams don't die when God gives them!

Honesty is where deliverance comes. Some of you feel like you'll never become anything. You can go on with your plastic smile and continue living bound by discouragement and depression. Or, you can be honest with yourself and say, "I need your deliverance, Jesus!" Let Jesus heal you. Let Him open that door that's been locked for so long. Your dream isn't dead. God will use you if you don't oversleep. Choose the freedom that can only come from forgiveness!

Endnotes

[i] OT:45199 Menashsheh (men-ash-sheh'); from OT:5382; causing to forget; Menashsheh, a grandson of Jacob, also the tribe descended from him, and its territory: (Biblesoft's New Exhaustive Strong's Numbers and Concordance with Expanded Greek-Hebrew Dictionary. Copyright © 1994, 2003, 2006 Biblesoft, Inc. and International Bible Translators, Inc.)

[ii] OT:669 Ephrayim (ef-rah'-yim); dual of masculine form of OT:672; double fruit; Ephrajim, a son of Joseph; also the tribe descended from him, and its territory: (Biblesoft's New Exhaustive Strong's Numbers and Concordance with Expanded Greek-Hebrew Dictionary. Copyright © 1994, 2003, 2006 Biblesoft, Inc. and International Bible Translators, Inc.)

[iii] Ibid

Acknowledgments

Thank you Daniel Koren from Neosho, Missouri for the hours of unselfish time you invested into the Kingdom of God typing this book from dictation. You are a special chosen vessel of the Lord and your investment is greatly valued.

To my sweet wife Andrea, thank you for modeling the principles of the book during the 16 years of our marriage. You will have a special crown in heaven for the grace by which you have served the kingdom of God at my side.

Most of all thank you to my Lord and Savior Jesus Christ for the Grace and Mercy He has shown through the years in empowering me to overcome the deep wounds that life has dealt me. May you receive all Honor and Glory in Jesus Name!